Review, Practice, & Mastery of

Y0-BRC-037

COMMON CORE
MATHEMATICS
STATE STANDARDS

Reviewers

Deanna Avery • Nantucket Public Schools • Nantucket, MA

Melinda Baer • Saddleback Valley Unified School District • Lake Forest, CA

Theresa Casto • Northern Wells Community Schools • Bluffton, IN

Christine Dolan • Marlborough Public Schools • Marlborough, MA

Rebecca Haas • Illinois Public School District • Aurora, IL

Angela Kulacz • Elmhurst Unit School District • Elmhurst, IL

Suzan A. Lambert • Rowan-Salisbury School District • Salisbury, NC

Louise Leon • Florence Township Schools • Florence, NJ

Aaron Moring-D'Angier • Cook County Schools • Chicago, IL

Bruce Rainwater • San Diego Unified • San Diego, CA

Shantell Toups • St. Mary Parish • Berwick, LA

Debbie Smith • Opp City Schools • Opp, AL

Cheryl Wild • Higley Unified School District • Gilbert, AZ

© 2015 **Perfection Learning**®

Please visit our Web site at:

www.perfectionlearning.com

When ordering this book, please specify:
ISBN 978-0-7891-8943-1 or **94191**

1 2 3 4 5 6 PP 18 17 16 15 14

Printed in the United States of America

To the Student

This book will help you review, practice, and master the Common Core State Standards for Mathematics. Here are the steps to follow to use this book.

1. Take the Tryout Test and check your answers. Use the chart at the bottom of this page to find out your strengths and weaknesses in the areas covered. Don't be discouraged if you don't get all the answers right or if you don't understand some questions. Remember the questions that are hard for you to answer. They will be the types of questions you need to work on the most.

2. Work through the lessons that follow the Tryout Test. Each lesson reviews example items and provides a practice test based on the Common Core State Standards. Fill in the Keeping Score chart on page 134 as you complete each practice test.

3. After completing all the lessons, take the Mastery Test. Your score on this test will show your understanding of the Common Core State Standards for Mathematics.

Units	Tryout Test Items	Mastery Test Items
1 Ratios and Proportional Relationships	1, 2, 3, 4, 5, 6, 7, 8, 9	1, 2, 3, 4, 5, 6, 7, 8, 9
2 Operations	10, 11, 12, 13, 14	10, 11, 12, 13, 14
3 Number Concepts	15, 16, 17, 18, 19, 20, 21, 22, 23, 24, 25	15, 16, 17, 18, 19, 20, 21, 22, 23, 24, 25
4 Expressions	26, 27, 28, 29, 30, 31, 32, 33	26, 27, 28, 29, 30, 31, 32, 33
5 Equations and Inequalities	34, 35, 36, 37, 38, 39, 40	34, 35, 36, 37, 38, 39, 42
6 Measurement and Geometry	41, 42, 43, 44, 46	40, 41, 43, 44, 45
7 Statistics	45, 47, 48, 49, 50, 51, 52, 53, 54, 55	46, 47, 48, 49, 50, 51, 52, 53, 54, 55

Table of Contents

Tips for Taking Tests. . . . . Inside Front Cover

To the Student. 2

Tryout Test Take this sample test to find out what you know and don't know 5

Unit 1 Ratios and Proportional Relationships

1 Understanding Ratio **[6.RP.1]** 14
2 Using Diagrams to Model Ratios **[6.RP.1, 6.RP.3]** 15
3 Rate **[6.RP.2, 6.RP.3a, 6.RP.3b]** 18
4 Unit Rate **[6.RP.2, 6.RP.3b]**. 20
5 Understanding Percent **[6.RP.3c]** 22
6 Percent Problems **[6.RP.3c]** 23
7 Converting Measurement Units **[6.RP.3d]** 25
Unit 1 Application **[6.RP.1, 6.RP.2, 6.RP.3b, 6.RP.3d]** 27
Test Practice Unit 1 29

Unit 2 Operations

1 Dividing with Fractions **[6.NS.1]** 33
2 Dividing Multi-Digit Numbers **[6.NS.2]**. 36
3 Adding and Subtracting Decimals **[6.NS.3]**. 37
4 Multiplying and Dividing Decimals **[6.NS.3]** 39
Unit 2 Application **[6.NS.2, 6.NS.3]** 41
Test Practice Unit 2 43

Unit 3 Number Concepts

1 Factors and Multiples **[6.NS.4]** 45
2 Factors and the Distributive Property **[6.NS.4]**. 46
3 Positive and Negative Numbers **[6.NS.5, 6.NS.6c]** 48
4 Rational Numbers **[6.NS.6c]**. 49
5 Opposites **[6.NS.6a]** 50
6 Ordered Pairs **[6.NS.6b, 6.NS.6c]** 51
7 Comparing and Ordering Rational Numbers **[6.NS.7a, 6.NS.7b]** . . . 54
8 Absolute Value **[6.NS.7c, 6.NS.7d]** 56
9 Absolute Value and Distance **[6.NS.8]** 57

continued

Table of Contents *continued*

Unit 3 Application **[6.NS.5, 6.NS.6a, 6.NS.6b, 6.NS.6c, 6.NS.8]** **58**
Test Practice Unit 3 . . . . **61**

Unit 4 Expressions

1 Exponents **[6.EE.1]** 65
2 Writing Expressions **[6.EE.2a, 6.EE.2b]** 66
3 Evaluating Expressions **[6.EE.2c]** 68
4 Using Formulas **[6.EE.2c]** 69
5 Equivalent Expressions **[6.EE.3, 6.EE.4]** 71
Unit 4 Application **[6.EE.2a, 6.EE.2b, 6.EE.2c, 6.EE.4]** 73
Test Practice Unit 4 75

Unit 5 Equations and Inequalities

1 Writing Equations **[6.EE.6, 6.EE.7]** 77
2 Solving Equations **[6.EE.5., 6.EE.7]** 78
3 Writing Inequalities **[6.EE.8]** 80
4 Solutions for Inequalities **[6.EE.5, 6.EE.8]** 81
5 Two-Variable Equations **[6.EE.6, 6.EE.9]** 82
Unit 5 Application **[6.EE.5, 6.EE.6, 6.EE.7, 6.EE.8, 6.EE.9]** . . . 85
Test Practice Unit 5 87

Unit 6 Measurement and Geometry

1 Area of Triangles **[6.G.1]** 90
2 Area of Quadrilaterals **[6.G.1]** 92
3 Area of Polygons **[6.G.1]** 94
4 Volume of Rectangular Prisms **[6.G.2]** 95
5 Polygons in the Coordinate Plane **[6.G.3]** 98
6 Surface Area **[6.G.4]** 101
Unit 6 Application **[6.G.1, 6.G.4]** 103
Test Practice Unit 6 105

Unit 7 Statistics

1 Statistical Questions **[6.SP.1]** 109
2 Measures of Center **[6.SP.2, 6.SP.3, 6.SP.5c]** 109
3 Measures of Variation **[6.SP.2, 6.SP.3, 6.SP.5c]** 111
4 Displaying and Summarizing Data **[6.SP.4, 6.SP.5a, 6.SP.5b, 6.SP.5d]** 114
Unit 7 Application **[6.SP.2, 6.SP.3, 6.SP.4, 6.SP.5b, 6.SP.5c, 6.SP.5d]** 120
Test Practice Unit 7 123

Mastery Test Take this sample test to find out what you've learned. 126
Keeping Score 134
Finding Percent 135

Tryout Test

Estimated time: 60 minutes

Directions: Read and answer each question.

1 The chess club has 8 girls and a total of 20 members. Write the ratio of girls to boys in simplest form.

Ⓐ 2 to 3

Ⓑ 3 to 2

Ⓒ 2 to 5

Ⓓ 5 to 2

2 Joelle wrote 9 pages in her diary in 1.5 hours. At what unit rate did she write in her diary?

Ⓐ 1.6 pages per hour

Ⓑ 6 pages per hour

Ⓒ 7.5 pages per hour

Ⓓ 8 pages per hour

3 Together, Adriana and Carlos have 56 balloons. Adriana has 16 balloons. What is the ratio of Adriana's balloons to Carlos's balloons?

Answer: _____

4 Shona drove 264 miles in 5.5 hours. At that rate, how far can she drive in 7 hours?

Answer: _____

5 Twenty-six out of the 40 members of the fishing club were at a meeting. What percent of the members were at the meeting?

Answer: _____

6 The table shows the ratio of hours to cans filled for a machine.

Hours	Cans Filled
2	14,000
4	
6	42,000
8	56,000

What number is missing in the table?

Answer: _____

7 Kaylee got a 15% raise. She now earns $23 an hour. How much did she earn per hour before the raise?

Answer: _____

8 A coat regularly priced at $188 is on sale for 25% off. What is the sale price? Show your work below.

Answer: _____

9 Which measure is equal to 850 grams?

Ⓐ 0.85 kg

Ⓑ 8.5 kg

Ⓒ 85 kg

Ⓓ 8,500 kg

GO ON

10 This diagram shows how many pieces $\frac{1}{6}$ yard long Deon can cut from a piece of rope that is $\frac{2}{3}$ of a yard long.

$\frac{1}{3}$		$\frac{1}{3}$		$\frac{1}{3}$	
$\frac{1}{6}$	$\frac{1}{6}$	$\frac{1}{6}$	$\frac{1}{6}$	$\frac{1}{6}$	$\frac{1}{6}$

Which division equation represents this diagram?

Ⓐ $\frac{2}{3} \div \frac{1}{6} = 4$

Ⓑ $\frac{1}{6} \div \frac{2}{3} = 4$

Ⓒ $\frac{2}{3} \div \frac{1}{6} = \frac{4}{6}$

Ⓓ $\frac{1}{6} \div 4 = \frac{2}{3}$

11 How many $\frac{1}{4}$-pound pieces of cheese can be cut from $\frac{5}{8}$ of a pound cheese? Draw a diagram to show the answer.

Answer: _____

12 A list of 782 names is divided equally into 34 columns. How many names are in each column?

Ⓐ 23

Ⓑ 32

Ⓒ 43

Ⓓ 230

13 Janeka sold 2 model airplanes. She packed the planes in boxes that weighed 0.85 pounds and 1.4 pounds. What was the total weight of the 2 boxes?

Answer: _____

14 Ruth Ann used 0.8 meters of cord to trim a picture frame. How many more frames of this size can she trim with 13.5 meters of additional cord?

Ⓐ 1.6   Ⓒ 16

Ⓑ 1.7   Ⓓ 17

15 What is the greatest common factor (GCF) of 36 and 40?

Ⓐ 2   Ⓒ 90

Ⓑ 4   Ⓓ 360

16 What is the least common multiple (LCM) of 9 and 6?

Answer: _____

17 Use the distributive property to write 49 + 14 as a sum with no common factors.

Answer: _____

18 The coldest temperature James ever recorded at his house was 14 degrees below zero. Write the number to show the temperature.

Answer: _____

19 Use this number line.

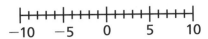

What is the opposite of 8?

Answer: _____

20 In which quadrant is point $(-1, 2)$ located?

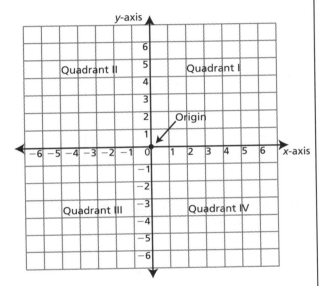

Answer: _____

21 What are the coordinates of the reflection of $(6, 5)$ over the y-axis?

Ⓐ $(6, -5)$

Ⓑ $(-6, 5)$

Ⓒ $(-6, -5)$

Ⓓ $(6, 5)$

22 Which inequality is shown by the points on this number line?

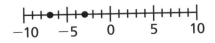

Ⓐ $-7 > -3$

Ⓑ $-3 > -7$

Ⓒ $7 < 3$

Ⓓ $3 < -7$

23 Which temperature is less than $-5°$ Fahrenheit?

Ⓐ $4°$ Ⓒ $0°$

Ⓑ $-3°$ Ⓓ $-8°$

24 What is $|-9|$?

Answer: _____

25 Use this grid to show the locations of monuments in Elmwood.

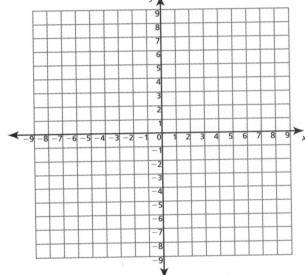

Soldier's Monument $(-6, -5)$

Founder's Monument $(5, 4)$

Liberty Monument $(-6, 6)$

Peace Monument $(-3, 4)$

The side of each square shows 1 mile.

A What is the distance from Liberty Monument to Soldier's Monument?

Answer: _____

B What is the distance from Peace Monument to Founder's Monument?

Answer: _____

GO ON

26 Which expression equals 5^4?

 Ⓐ 4×5

 Ⓑ $5 \times 4 \times 5 \times 4$

 Ⓒ $5 \times 5 \times 5 \times 5$

 Ⓓ $4 \times 4 \times 4 \times 4 \times 4$

27 Which expression represents 25 less than double a number n?

 Ⓐ $25 - 2n$ Ⓒ $2(25 - n)$

 Ⓑ $2n - 25$ Ⓓ $2(n - 25)$

28 What is the constant in the expression $3m + 7$?

 Answer: _____

29 The formula for the area of a triangle is $A = \frac{1}{2}bh$. Use the formula to find the area of a triangle with a base (b) of 10 inches and a height (h) of 18 inches.

 Ⓐ 9 in.^{2} Ⓒ 90 in.^{2}

 Ⓑ 18 in.^{2} Ⓓ 180 in.^{2}

30 What is the value of the expression below when $k = 5$ and $m = 10$? Show your work below.

$$(9k + 8m) \div 5$$

 Answer: _____

31 Simplify this expression.

$$56 \div 7 + 3 \times 5 - 4^2$$

 Answer: _____

32 Which expression is equivalent to $56n - 24t$?

 Ⓐ $7 \times 8(n - t)$

 Ⓑ $7(8n - 4t)$

 Ⓒ $8(7n - 3t)$

 Ⓓ $8 \times 3(n - t)$

33 Simplify this expression.

$$9y + 2 + 4y$$

 Ⓐ $13y + 2$ Ⓒ $11y + 2$

 Ⓑ $15y$ Ⓓ $13y^2 + 2$

34 Which value of x makes the inequality $x < -4$ true?

 Ⓐ -8

 Ⓑ -4

 Ⓒ 0

 Ⓓ 2

35 How can you solve the equation $15 + x = 32$?

 Ⓐ Add 32 to both sides.

 Ⓑ Subtract 32 from both sides.

 Ⓒ Add 15 to both sides.

 Ⓓ Subtract 15 from both sides.

36 Julia bought 3 lamps. She paid a total of $396. Which equation can be used to find the amount she paid for each lamp?

 Ⓐ $3 \times l = \$396$

 Ⓑ $\$396 \times l = 3$

 Ⓒ $3 \div l = \$396$

 Ⓓ $\$396 = l + 3$

37 Solve for *p*.

$$16 \times p = 96$$

Ⓐ $p = 1{,}536$

Ⓑ $p = 12$

Ⓒ $p = 6$

Ⓓ $p = 4$

38 To ride on the Wild Whip at the fair a person must be at least 48 inches tall. Write an inequality to show the height, *h*.

Answer: _____

39 Which number line shows the solution set for the inequality $m < 2$?

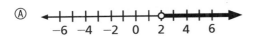

Ⓐ

Ⓑ

Ⓒ

Ⓓ

40 James started with $180 in his savings account.

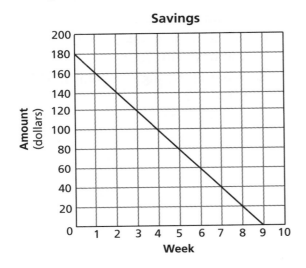

Make a table to show the relationship between the number of weeks (*w*) and the amount of savings (*s*). Then write an equation. Show your work and explain your answer.

Week (*w*)	Savings (*s*)

Equation: _____

Explanation: _____

_____

_____

_____

_____

_____

GO ON

41 Find the area of this polygon and explain how you arrived at your answer.

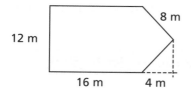

Answer: _____

_____

_____

_____

_____

42 Ricardo wants to find the area of this shape so he can figure out how much paint to buy to cover it. What is the area of the shape?

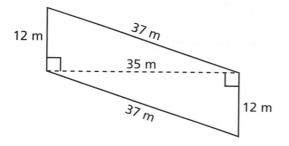

- Ⓐ 210 m^2
- Ⓑ 420 m^2
- Ⓒ 444 m^2
- Ⓓ 1,295 m^2

43 A box of candles is $\frac{1}{2}$ inch tall, $2\frac{3}{4}$ inches wide, and 3 inches long. What is the volume of the box?

Answer: _____

44 Plot the points $(-4, 5)$, $(3, 5)$, $(3, -4)$, and $(-4, -4)$ on this coordinate grid. Connect the points in order.

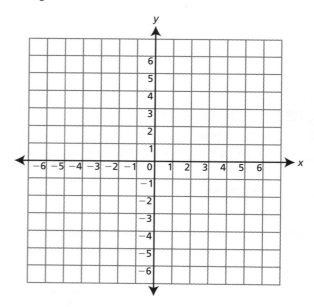

What is the perimeter of the quadrilateral?

Answer: _____

45 Troy teaches mountain climbing. He asked the members of his class these questions. Which is a statistical question?

- Ⓐ What is the elevation of the highest point on Mount McKinley?
- Ⓑ How many people are in this mountain-climbing class?
- Ⓒ What is the greatest height to which you have climbed?
- Ⓓ What is the highest point in this county?

46 Alden built this prism using 1 cm cubes.

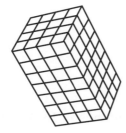

Draw a net of the prism. Then find its surface area. Show your work.

Answer: _____

Ralph kept track of the number of minutes he worked out last week. Use Ralph's data to answer questions 48–50.

Workouts (minutes)				
50	45	70	65	50

48 What is the range of the times?

Ⓐ 20 minutes

Ⓑ 25 minutes

Ⓒ 30 minutes

Ⓓ 70 minutes

49 What is the mean time?

Ⓐ 50 minutes

Ⓑ 55 minutes

Ⓒ 56 minutes

Ⓓ 68 minutes

50 What is the mean absolute deviation for the times?

Ⓐ 46 minutes

Ⓑ 14 minutes

Ⓒ 9.2 minutes

Ⓓ 4.6 minutes

47 Ahmed recorded the number of math problems he did for homework each day. Here are his numbers.

25, 15, 31, 33, 26, 29, 27, 31, 38, 40,

12, 35, 29, 27, 33, 45, 19, 26, 52, 10

What is the median of the data?

Ⓐ 27   Ⓒ 29

Ⓑ 28   Ⓓ 29.5

51 Which describes the center of a set of data?

Ⓐ range

Ⓑ outlier

Ⓒ median

Ⓓ mean absolute deviation

52 The range of points scored by the Cougars in their basketball games is 18. Which statement is true?

Ⓐ All scores were greater than 18 points.

Ⓑ The scores varied by an average of 18 points.

Ⓒ The middle score for all of the games was 18 points.

Ⓓ The difference between the highest and lowest score was 18 points.

53 For which box plot are the values for the middle half of the data closest together?

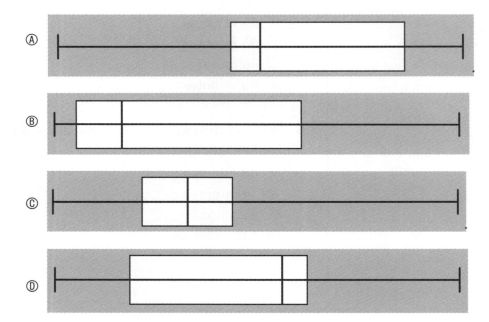

The histogram shows the ages of members of a surf club. Use the histogram for questions 54 and 55.

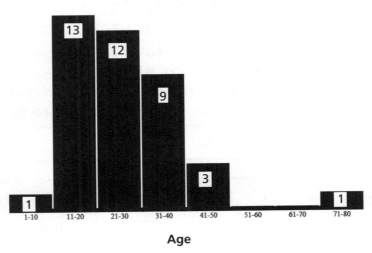

Ages of Surf Club Members

Age

54 How many members does the surf club have?

Answer: _____

55 Which describes the shape of the data?

Ⓐ normal

Ⓑ skewed

Ⓒ uniform with an outlier

Ⓓ skewed with an outlier

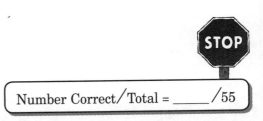

Number Correct／Total = _____ ／55

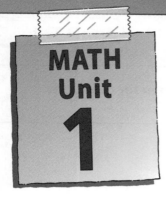

MATH Unit 1

Ratios and Proportional Relationships

1 Understanding Ratio [**6.RP.1**]
2 Using Diagrams to Model Ratios [**6.RP.1, 6.RP.3**]
3 Rate [**6.RP.2, 6.RP.3a, 6.RP.3b**]
4 Unit Rate [**6.RP.2, 6.RP.3b**]
5 Understanding Percent [**6.RP.3c**]
6 Percent Problems [**6.RP.3c**]
7 Converting Measurement Units [**6.RP.3d**]
Unit 1 Application [**6.RP.1, 6.RP.2, 6.RP.3b, 6.RP.3d**]

Directions: Read and answer each question.

Understanding Ratio

1   What is the ratio of squares to circles?

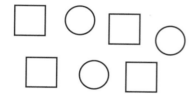

   Ⓐ 4 : 3   Ⓒ 3 : 7

   Ⓑ 3 : 4   Ⓓ 4 : 7

Step-By-Step

Example 1 is a ratio problem. A **ratio** compares two quantities, such as the squares and circles in this example. Follow these steps.

1   First record the number of circles and squares.

Squares: ⬜️   Circles: ⬜️

2   You can express *the ratio of squares to circles* in three ways.

    With words: 4 to 3
    As a fraction: $\frac{4}{3}$
    With a colon: 4 : 3

Understanding Ratio

2 What is the ratio of circles to the total number of shapes?

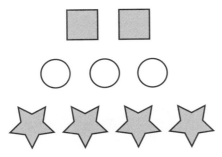

Ⓐ $\frac{3}{4}$

Ⓑ $\frac{1}{2}$

Ⓒ $\frac{2}{3}$

Ⓓ $\frac{1}{3}$

Using Diagrams to Model Ratios

3 The ratio of the number of crayons Jenny has to the number of crayons Ed has is 4 to 5. If Jenny has 24 crayons, how many crayons does Ed have?

Answer: _____

Step-By-Step

Example 2 asks you to find the ratio of a part to the whole. Follow these steps.

1 How many circles are there?

2 How many shapes are there in all?

3 Write the ratio as a fraction.

4 Simplify a ratio the same way you simplify a fraction—divide both terms by the same factor.

$$\frac{3 \div 3}{9 \div 3} = \frac{}{}$$

Step-By-Step

You can draw a model of the ratio 4 to 5 to help you find the answer to **example 3**.

1 Draw 4 blocks to show Jenny's crayons. Draw 5 blocks to show Ed's crayons. Label each model.

|-- 24 crayons --|

Jenny's Crayons

Ed's Crayons

|----------- c -----------|

2 Jenny's 4 blocks show 24 crayons. Divide to find the number of crayons shown by 1 block.

4 blocks = 24 crayons

1 block = 24 ÷ 4 = ☐ crayons

3 Ed's crayons are shown by 5 blocks. Each block shows 6 crayons. Multiply to find the number of crayons Ed has.

5 blocks = 5 × 6 = ☐ crayons

4 The ratio of yellow tulip bulbs to red tulip bulbs in a package is 2 to 3. There are 100 tulip bulbs in the package. How many of each color bulb are there?

Answer: _____ yellow, _____ red

Step-By-Step

Draw a diagram to help you find the answer for **example 4**.

1 Draw a line to show the total number of bulbs.

$$\text{100}$$
|————————————|

2 The ratio of yellow to red bulbs is 2 to 3. So for every 5 bulbs, 2 are yellow and 3 are red. Divide the line into 5 equal pieces. Label 2 pieces *yellow*. Label 3 pieces *red*.

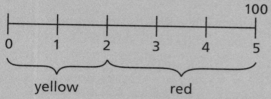

3 Divide 100 by 5 to find the value of each section of the number line.

$$100 \div 5 = \boxed{}$$

4 To find the number of each color bulb, multiply its number of sections by 20.

$$\text{Yellow} = 2 \times 20 = \boxed{}$$

$$\text{Red} = 3 \times 20 = \boxed{}$$

Try It

1 José and Tia are selling candles for a fund-raiser. Tia has earned $15 to José's $20. What is her ratio of earnings to his?

Answer: _____

2 Josh's class sold 200 tickets to raise money for a new park. Three tickets were drawn and those people received prizes. Write the ratio of winners to total tickets sold.

Answer: _____

3 A rug is 6 feet wide and 10 feet long. What is the ratio of the length to the width?

   Ⓐ 3 : 5   Ⓒ 3 : 8

   Ⓑ 5 : 3   Ⓓ 8 : 3

4 In Jaleel's chess club, 3 out of every 8 members are girls. What is the ratio of boys to girls in the club?

   Ⓐ 3 to 8

   Ⓑ 8 to 3

   Ⓒ 5 to 8

   Ⓓ 5 to 3

Questions 5–6: Complete each ratio so that it will be equivalent to a ratio of 3 : 4.

5 30 to _____

6 _____ to 16

5 Soup costs $10 for 3 cans. Josh spent $40 on soup. How many cans did he buy?

Answer: _____

Think It Through

One way to find equal ratios as in **example 5** is to make a table. Multiply both the number of cans and the price by 2, 3, 4, and so on.

	Cans of Soup	Price
	3	$10
Times 2	6	$20
Times 3	9	
Times 4	12	

Use the table to answer the question.

6 A sixth-grade class is putting on a car wash to raise money for a trip. This table shows the number of cars they had washed at the end of each of the first 4 hours.

Hours	Cars Washed
1	10
2	20
3	30
4	40

If they continue washing cars at the same rate, how many cars will they have washed in 8 hours?

Answer: _____

Step-By-Step

For **example 6** compare the hours to the number of cars washed and look for a pattern.

1 1 hour: 10 cars $10 \times 1 = 10$
   2 hours: 20 cars $10 \times 2 = 20$
   3 hours: 30 cars $10 \times 3 = 30$
   4 hours: 40 cars $10 \times 4 = 40$

   The number of cars washed is _____ times the number of hours.

2 Multiply 10 times the number of hours to find the number of cars that the students can wash in 8 hours.

   _____ $\times$ _____ = _____ cars

Open-Ended Practice

Some tests include open-ended questions in which you must show your work and write an explanation of the steps you took. There is often more than one answer or more than one way to find a solution to these problems.

Rate

7 A recipe calls for grape juice and apple juice in a ratio of 3 cups to 5 cups. To the nearest cup, estimate the amount of grape juice Barry should use if he has 16 cups of apple juice.

Show OR describe each step of your work, even if you do it in your head ("mental math") or use a calculator.

Explanation: _____

_____

_____

_____

_____

Step-By-Step

Plan how you will find the number of cups of grape juice for **example 7**. Then show your work and explain your thinking.

My Plan: *I will make a table of equivalent ratios. I will plot the ordered pairs formed by the ratios on the coordinate plane. Then I can use the graph to estimate the number of cups of grape juice Barry should use.*

1 Make a table of ratios equivalent to 3:5 and write them as ordered pairs.

3:5	(3,5)
6:10	(6,10)
9:15	(9,15)
12:20	(12,20)
15:25	(15,25)

2 Plot the points and draw a line connecting them.

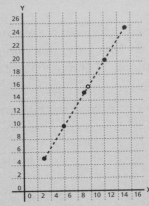

3 Locate the point on the line that has 16 as the *y*-value. Estimate the *x*-value to estimate the number of cups of grape juice.

For 16 cups of apple juice, use about ⬚ cups of grape juice.

Explanation: *The x-value for the point with y-value 16 is between 9 and 10. It is closer to 10, so I used 10 as my estimate.*

GO ON ⟩

8 The veterinarian put Jeremy's dog Spot
   on a diet. On the diet, Spot lost
   15 pounds in 60 days. At what unit rate
   did Spot lose weight?

   Ⓐ 0.25 pounds per day

   Ⓑ 0.5 pounds per day

   Ⓒ 2 pounds per day

   Ⓓ 4 pounds per day

Remember . . .

A **rate** is a ratio that compares two
unlike units such as **dollars** and
pounds.

A **unit rate** shows the rate for one unit.

5 pounds of apples cost $2.00

The unit rate for apples is $0.40 per pound.

9 Marcie planted 3 tomato plants in
   45 minutes. At this rate, how long will it
   take her to plant 14 tomato plants?

   Answer: _____

Step-By-Step

To solve **example 8**, write a ratio to
compare pounds lost to days. Then find
the unit rate.

1 Write a ratio using pounds lost as the
   numerator and days as the denominator.

   $$\frac{\boxed{}\ \text{pounds}}{\boxed{}\ \text{days}}$$

2 Divide the numerator and the
   denominator by 60 to find the unit rate.

   $$\frac{15}{60} = \frac{(15 \div 60)}{(60 \div 60)} = \boxed{}\ \text{pounds/day}$$

Step-By-Step

For **example 9**, first find the unit rate,
or the amount of time it takes Marcie to
plant 1 tomato plant.

1 Divide 45 minutes by 3 to find the unit
   rate.

   $$45 \div 3 = \boxed{}\ \text{minutes}$$

2 Multiply the unit rate by 14 to find the
   time needed to plant 14 tomato plants.

   $$15 \times 14 = \boxed{}\ \text{minutes}$$

7 Paul took a 42-mile bicycle trip. He bicycled $1\frac{1}{2}$ hours in the morning and 2 hours in the afternoon. What was his average speed in miles per hour?

Answer: _____

8 Dish soap comes in two sizes: 18 oz for 69¢ and 24 oz for $1.28. Which size is the better buy?

Answer: _____

9 A sailboat sailed for $3\frac{1}{4}$ hours at an average speed of 8 knots and then for 3 more hours at 5 knots. (1 knot is equal to 1 nautical mile per hour.) How far did the boat sail?

Answer: _____

10 How can you find the unit price for trail mix if you know that someone paid $2.78 for 8 ounces?

Ⓐ Multiply $2.78 by 8.

Ⓑ Subtract 8 from $2.78.

Ⓒ Divide $2.78 by 8.

Ⓓ Divide 8 by $2.78.

11 On a fishing trip, Camie and her friends covered 77 miles at an average speed of 28 miles per hour. How long did this trip take?

Ⓐ $1\frac{3}{4}$ hours   Ⓒ $2\frac{1}{2}$ hours

Ⓑ $2\frac{1}{4}$ hours   Ⓓ $2\frac{3}{4}$ hours

12 Yola paid $20 for 8.7 gallons of gas. Victor paid $30 for 12.4 gallons. Compare the price per gallon to find out who got the better buy.

Yola: _____

Victor: _____

13 Penelope spent $4.26 for 3 pounds of potato salad. What was the price per pound?

Answer: _____

14 Philip can run a mile in 6 minutes. What is his speed in miles per hour?

Ⓐ 6 mi/hr   Ⓒ 12 mi/hr

Ⓑ 10 mi/hr   Ⓓ 60 mi/hr

15 Dried herbs come in two sizes. Which is the better buy—30 grams for $2.45, or 48 grams for $3.67?

Answer: _____

16 Walter drove a distance of 120 miles in 3 hours. By how much must he increase the speed to cover the distance in 2.4 hours?

Ⓐ 10 mi/hr   Ⓒ 40 mi/hr

Ⓑ 30 mi/hr   Ⓓ 50 mi/hr

17 Paula bicycled for 20 minutes and covered 5 miles. What is her speed in miles per hour?

Answer: _____

GO ON

10 What percent of this grid is shaded?

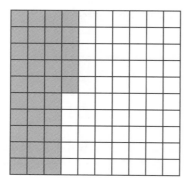

Ⓐ 35%   Ⓒ 65%

Ⓑ 53%   Ⓓ 32%

11 What percent of this circle is shaded?

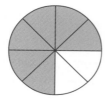

Ⓐ 68%   Ⓒ 75%

Ⓑ 26%   Ⓓ 86%

Remember . . .

To change a fraction to a decimal, divide the numerator by the denominator.

$$\frac{7}{8} = 7 \div 8 = 0.875$$

Step-By-Step

A **percent** is a ratio in which the first term is compared to 100. Therefore, a fraction with a denominator of 100 can be written as an equivalent percent. For **example 10**, first write a ratio for the number of shaded squares.

1 35 out of 100 squares are shaded. Write the ratio as a fraction.

2 Write the fraction as a percent.

$$\frac{35}{100} = \boxed{} \%$$

For **example 11** follow these steps to see another way to write a fraction as an equivalent percent.

1 In the circle, 6 out of 8 sections are shaded. Write the ratio as a simplified fraction.

$$\frac{6}{8} = \boxed{}$$

2 Write the fraction as an equivalent decimal.

$$\frac{3}{4} = 0.75$$

3 To convert a decimal to percent, move the decimal point two places to the right.

$$0.75 = \boxed{} \%$$

Percent Problems

12 Juan bought an $80 coat on sale for $60. What percent of the original price did he save?

Ⓐ 25%

Ⓑ 40%

Ⓒ 60%

Ⓓ 75%

13 The regular price of a dishwasher is $350. Jeff bought one on sale at a 30% discount. How much did Jeff pay for the dishwasher?

Ⓐ $455   Ⓒ $245

Ⓑ $345   Ⓓ $105

Another Way

Subtract the percent discount from 100%. Then multiply the regular price by the difference as a decimal.

$$100\% - 30\% = 70\% = 0.7$$
$$0.7 \times \$350 = \$245$$

Step-By-Step

To solve **example 12**, first find the amount saved. Then divide it by the original price to find the percent.

1 Find the amount saved.

$$\$80 - \$60 = \boxed{}$$

2 Divide.

$$\frac{20}{80} = 20 \div 80 = \boxed{}$$

3 Change your answer to a percent.

$$0.25 = \boxed{} \%$$

Step-By-Step

To solve **example 13**, first compute the amount of the discount, and then subtract that amount from the regular price.

1 Compute the amount of the discount.

Write 30% as a decimal.
$$30\% = 0.3$$
$$0.3 \times \$350 = \boxed{}$$

2 Subtract the discount from the regular price.

$$\$350 - \boxed{} = \boxed{}$$

GO ON

Percent Problems

14 At a 20% off sale, Paula paid $48 for a sweater. What was the original price of the sweater?

Answer: _____

Another Way

Draw a diagram to help you solve the problem.

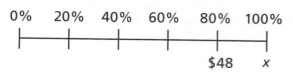

0%   20%   40%   60%   80%   100%

$48   x

Step-By-Step

For **example 14**, you want to find 100% of the cost of the sweater.

1 The price Paula paid is 20% off the original price. Subtract to find the percent of the original price that Paula paid.

$$100\% - 20\% = \boxed{}$$

2 80% of the original price is $48. Let p be the original price. Write an equation showing that 80% of p is $48.

$$80\% \times p = \boxed{}$$

3 Change 80% to a decimal. Solve for p.

$$0.80 \times p = 48$$

$$p = 48 \div 0.80$$

$$p = \boxed{}$$

Try It

18 The regular price of a sewing machine is $450. Nevin found one for sale at a 20% discount. How much did Nevin pay for the sewing machine? Write your answer on the line.

Answer: _____

19 Four friends had dinner. The total bill was $35. They left a 20% tip. How much was the tip?

Answer: _____

20 Pete bought an $80 coat on sale for $70. What percent of the price did he save?

  Ⓐ 12.5%   Ⓒ 10%
  Ⓑ 8%   Ⓓ 70%

21 Find 30% of $450.

Answer: _____

22 About what percent of the people shown on this graph chose baseball?

  Ⓐ 25%   Ⓒ 10%
  Ⓑ 30%   Ⓓ 50%

23 A drawing is 18 centimeters tall and 10 centimeters wide. Tina reduced the drawing 30% to make it fit on a scrapbook page. How wide is the reduced drawing?

   Ⓐ 3 cm   Ⓒ 12.6 cm

   Ⓑ 5.4 cm   Ⓓ 7 cm

24 Regular price for concert tickets is $24. Students pay $18. What percent is the student discount?

   Answer: _____

25 At Lauren's school, 60% of the students own calculators. There are 250 students in the school. How many own calculators?

   Ⓐ 15   Ⓒ 150

   Ⓑ 60   Ⓓ 180

26 A television usually costs $150. During a sale, its price is reduced 6%. What is the price during the sale?

   Answer: _____

Questions 27–30: Calculate 10% of each quantity.

27 16 yd _____

28 $43 _____

29 $\frac{1}{2}$ lb _____

30 128 grams _____

Converting Measurement Units

15 Bob bought 4.3 kilograms of fancy nuts. How many grams did he buy?

   Ⓐ 0.43 grams   Ⓒ 430 grams

   Ⓑ 43 grams   Ⓓ 4,300 grams

Changing Units

Multiply to change from a larger unit to a smaller unit.

Divide to change from a smaller unit to a larger unit.

Think It Through

For **example 15** the ratio of kilograms to grams is 1 to 1,000.

$$1 \text{ kilogram} = 1,000 \text{ grams}$$

A kilogram is larger than a gram, so to convert 4.3 kilograms to grams, multiply 4.3 by 1,000.

$$4.3 \times 1,000 = \boxed{} \text{ grams}$$

Converting Measurement Units

16 Laura bought 324 inches of ribbon. How many yards of ribbon did she buy?

Ⓐ 9 yards

Ⓑ 18 yards

Ⓒ 27 yards

Ⓓ 108 yards

Step-By-Step

To convert between units of measurement, multiply or divide by the correct conversion factor. Check the *Table of Common Measurements* box below.

1 First write the conversion factor; then write the problem to be solved. Be sure to put like items on the same side of both equations as shown below.

$$1 \text{ yard} = 36 \text{ inches}$$

$$\underline{?} \text{ yards} = 324 \text{ inches}$$

2 The conversion factor is 36. Since *inch* is a smaller unit than *yard*, you will need to divide 324 by 36 to convert yards to inches.

$$324 \div 36 = \boxed{} \text{ yards}$$

Table of Common Measurements

1 minute (min) = 60 seconds (sec)

1 hour (hr) = 60 minutes (min)

1 day (d) = 24 hours (hr)

1 week (wk) = 7 days (d)

1 year = 365 days (d)

1 year = 52 weeks (wk)

1 year = 12 months (mo)

1 foot (ft) = 12 inches (in.)

1 yard (yd) = 36 inches (in.)

1 yard (yd) = 3 feet (ft)

1 mile (mi) = 5,280 feet (ft)

1 pound (lb) = 16 ounces (oz)

1 ton (T) = 2,000 pounds (lb)

1 cup (c) = 8 fluid ounces (fl oz)

1 pint (pt) = 2 cups (c)

1 quart (qt) = 2 pints (pt)

1 gallon (gal) = 4 quarts (qt)

1 liter (L) = 1,000 milliliters (mL)

1 centimeter (cm) = 10 millimeters (mm)

1 meter (m) = 100 centimeters (cm)

1 kilometer (km) = 1,000 meters (m)

1 gram (g) = 1,000 milligrams (mg)

1 kilogram (kg) = 1,000 grams (g)

1 metric ton (t) = 1,000 kilograms (kg)

17 John is running a race. He knows he can run 60 feet in 4 seconds. If he maintains this rate, how many miles will he run in 1 hour? Show all of your work.

Step 1

$$\frac{\boxed{}\text{ feet}}{\boxed{}\text{ seconds}} = \boxed{}\text{ per second}$$

John's unit rate is $\boxed{}$ feet/second.

Step 2

$$\frac{\boxed{}\text{ feet}}{\boxed{}\text{ second}} \times \frac{60\text{ seconds}}{1\text{ minute}} = \frac{\boxed{}\text{ feet}}{\boxed{}\text{ minutes}} = \boxed{}\text{ ft/min}$$

John can run $\boxed{}$ feet in 1 minute.

Step 3

$$\frac{\boxed{}\text{ feet}}{\boxed{}\text{ minute}} \times \frac{60\text{ minutes}}{1\text{ hour}} = \frac{\boxed{}\text{ feet}}{\boxed{}\text{ hours}} = \boxed{}\text{ ft/hr}$$

John can run $\boxed{}$ feet in 1 hour.

Step 4

$$\frac{\boxed{}\text{ feet}}{\boxed{}\text{ hour}} \times \frac{1\text{ mile}}{5,280\text{ feet}} = \frac{\boxed{}\text{ miles}}{\boxed{}\text{ hours}} = \boxed{}\text{ mi/hr}$$

Answer: _____

Step-By-Step

This problem involves several steps. The first step is to find John's unit rate. **Remember:** A rate is a ratio that compares two unlike units.

1 First I'll find the unit rate. John's rate is 60 feet in 4 seconds, so I divide 60 feet by 4 seconds to determine his unit rate.

2 Since I am solving for John's speed in miles per hour, I need to convert seconds to an hour. First I'll convert seconds to minutes.

3 Next I convert minutes to hours.

4 Now I know how many feet John can run in an hour. But I want to know how many miles he can run in an hour. So I convert feet to miles. There are 5,280 feet in a mile.

31 If you watch an hour-long television show without the commercials, the show lasts 45 minutes. One television network is talking about changing the ratio of commercials to show time to 2:8. Draw two diagrams, one that shows the current ratio and one that shows the proposed ratio. If this change is made, does the amount of time dedicated to commercials increase?

Answer: _____

32 Annie can run 13 miles in 2.5 hours. How many feet can she run in 1 second? Show your work below.

Answer: _____

Go for it!

Test Practice 1: Ratios and Proportional Relationships

Estimated time: 25 minutes

Directions: Read and answer each question.

1 What percent of this square is shaded?

Ⓐ 65%　　　Ⓒ 68%
Ⓑ 66%　　　Ⓓ 70%

2 Josh scored 3 goals out of 10 attempts in today's soccer game. What percent of the time did Josh make a goal?

Ⓐ 30%　　　Ⓒ $3\frac{1}{3}$%
Ⓑ 10%　　　Ⓓ 3%

3 What is the ratio of cars to trucks?

Ⓐ 3 : 8　　　Ⓒ 5 : 8
Ⓑ 5 : 3　　　Ⓓ 3 : 5

4 Gail is competing in a checkers tournament. She won 12 out of a total of 20 games. What is her ratio of wins to losses?

Ⓐ 3 : 5　　　Ⓒ 5 : 3
Ⓑ 3 : 2　　　Ⓓ 2 : 3

5 In Sharla's computer club, 4 out of every 7 members are girls. What is the ratio of boys to girls in the club?

Ⓐ 3 to 7　　　Ⓒ 4 to 3
Ⓑ 7 to 3　　　Ⓓ 3 to 4

6 Chiu-Ling bought 8.3 meters of string. How many centimeters of string did she buy?

Ⓐ 8,300 centimeters
Ⓑ 830 centimeters
Ⓒ 83 centimeters
Ⓓ 0.83 centimeter

7 Mr. Ford drove 224 miles in 4 hours. At what rate of speed did he drive?

Answer: _____

8 Jordan drank 36 ounces of water today. How many cups of water did he drink?

Ⓐ 4.5 cups　　　Ⓒ 18 cups
Ⓑ 9 cups　　　Ⓓ 288 cups

9 Mr. Liston bought lunch for $12.80. He gave the waiter a tip of 15%. How much money did the waiter receive?

Ⓐ $1.28
Ⓑ $1.92
Ⓒ $2.56
Ⓓ $3.84

10 Devin wants to buy a book that costs $28.99. He has a coupon for 30% off the price of the book. If Devin uses his coupon, about how much money will he save?

Ⓐ $0.30　　　　Ⓒ $9

Ⓑ $1　　　　　Ⓓ $21

11 The table shows the ratio of hours to cakes baked at a bakery.

Hours	Cakes Baked
1	
3	48
6	96
8	128

What number is missing in the table?

Answer: _____

12 Maria usually pays $3.10 per pound for her favorite granola. Which of the answers below is a better deal?

Ⓐ 2 pounds for $6.49

Ⓑ 3 pounds for $10

Ⓒ 5 pounds for $14.75

Ⓓ 8 pounds for $28

13 Ten fence posts cost $92. Mr. Bell spent $276 for fence posts. How many did he buy?

Answer: _____

14 Dirk recorded the hair color of every student in his class. He made this circle graph to show his results.

Hair Color Survey Results

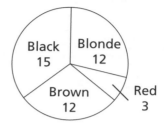

What is the ratio of the number of students with blonde or red hair to the number of students with black or brown hair?

Ⓐ 5 : 9　　　　Ⓒ 3 : 1

Ⓑ 1 : 3　　　　Ⓓ 9 : 5

15 The ratio of peanuts to cashews in a mix is 5 to 7. How many ounces of peanuts are there in a 48-ounce jar of the mix?

Answer: _____

16 Look at the rate table below. What will the temperature be at 11:00 a.m. if the temperature continues to rise at the same rate?

Time (A.M.)	7	8	9	10
Temperature	55°	58°	61°	64°

Ⓐ 66°　　　　Ⓒ 68°

Ⓑ 67°　　　　Ⓓ 70°

17 Jake earned $62.50 in 5 hours. At the same rate, how much will he earn in 8 hours?

Answer: _____

18 The ratio of cats to dogs at the animal shelter is 3 to 5. There are 27 cats. How many dogs are there?

Answer: _____

19 What percent of the circle is NOT shaded?

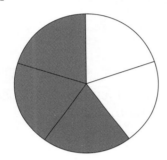

Ⓐ 40%

Ⓑ 30%

Ⓒ 20%

Ⓓ 25%

20 Grapes are priced at 2 pounds for $3. Complete the table to show the price of various weights. Then plot the data on the coordinate grid.

Weight (in pounds)	Price
2	$3
4	$6
6	
8	
10	

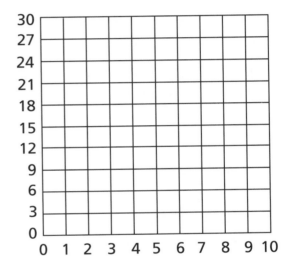

Use your graph. About how many pounds of grapes can you buy for $8?

Answer: _____

GO ON

21 Alice is trying to find out how far she could walk in 2 hours, if she can walk 10 feet in 3 seconds. Show your work.

Answer: _____

22 Luna can sew 10 feet of fabric in 4 minutes.

Part A: First determine Luna's unit rate. How many feet of fabric can Luna sew in 1 minute?

Answer: _____

Part B: How many feet of fabric can Luna sew in an hour?

Answer: _____

Part C: How many yards of fabric can she sew in an hour?

Answer: _____

STOP

Number Correct/Total = _____/22

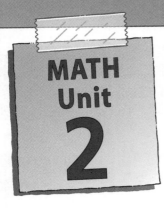

MATH Unit 2

Operations

1 Dividing with Fractions [**6.NS.1**]

2 Dividing Multi-Digit Numbers [**6.NS.2**]

3 Adding and Subtracting Decimals [**6.NS.3**]

4 Multiplying and Dividing Decimals [**6.NS.3**]

Unit 2 Application [**6.NS.2, 6.NS.3**]

Directions: Read and answer each question.

Dividing with Fractions

1 How many $\frac{3}{16}$-yard pieces can be cut from $\frac{3}{4}$ yard of ribbon?

Answer: _____

Try It

1 Small metal parts each measure $\frac{3}{16}$ of an inch. How many of these parts can be cut from a strip of metal that is 30 inches long? Show your work below.

Answer: _____

Step-By-Step

One way to divide $\frac{3}{4}$ of a yard into $\frac{3}{16}$-yard pieces for **example 1** is to draw a model.

1 To model $\frac{3}{4}$, draw a bar and divide it into 4 equal pieces. Shade 3 of the 4 pieces.

2 Divide the same bar into 16 pieces. Then draw brackets to show $\frac{3}{16}$-inch pieces. Count the number of $\frac{3}{16}$ pieces in $\frac{3}{4}$.

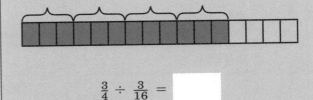

$$\frac{3}{4} \div \frac{3}{16} = \boxed{}$$

2 Arnold bought $2\frac{3}{4}$ yards of string. He needs to cut it into pieces $\frac{1}{4}$ yard long. How many pieces can he get?

Answer: _____

Dividing with Fractions

2 Find the quotient.

$$\frac{2}{3} \div \frac{3}{4} = \square$$

Answer: _____

Checking Division

Remember, multiplication and division are inverse operations, so you can check division by multiplying.

$$\frac{2}{3} \div \frac{3}{4} = \frac{8}{9}$$

Check:

$$\frac{8}{9} \times \frac{3}{4} = \frac{24}{36} = \frac{2}{3}$$

Try It

3 Five friends shared $8\frac{1}{3}$ pounds of apples equally. How many pounds of apples did each person get?

Answer: _____

4 $1\frac{3}{5} \div \frac{2}{3} =$

    Ⓐ $2\frac{2}{5}$ Ⓒ $1\frac{1}{15}$

    Ⓑ $1\frac{2}{5}$ Ⓓ $\frac{15}{16}$

5 $3 \div \frac{1}{6} =$ _____

6 How many $\frac{3}{4}$-inch pieces of wood can be cut from a strip 15 inches long?

Answer: _____

Step-By-Step

For **example 2**, make the fractions have the same denominator so the model is easy to draw.

1 Rewrite the fractions with a common denominator.

$$\frac{2}{3} = \frac{2 \times 4}{3 \times 4} = \square$$

$$\frac{3}{4} = \frac{3 \times 3}{4 \times 3} = \square$$

2 To divide $\frac{8}{12}$ by $\frac{9}{12}$, start by drawing a bar model for 1 whole and shading $\frac{8}{12}$ of it.

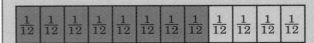

3 Draw a bracket to show $\frac{9}{12}$ of the whole.

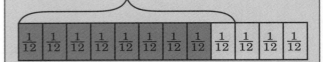

4 The number of times $\frac{9}{12}$ can be divided into $\frac{8}{12}$ is a fraction. The number of shaded sections is the numerator and the number of bracketed sections is the denominator.

$$\frac{8}{12} \div \frac{9}{12} = \frac{\boxed{}}{9}$$

$$\frac{2}{3} \div \frac{3}{4} = \square$$

Dividing with Fractions

3 An art class is painting a mural. The teacher has $\frac{5}{8}$ gallon of paint. Each student needs $\frac{1}{16}$ gallon to paint a part of the mural. How many students can paint?

   Ⓐ 5 students   Ⓒ 10 students

   Ⓑ 8 students   Ⓓ 16 students

Dividing by Fractions

To divide by a fraction, multiply by the reciprocal of the divisor.

$$\frac{1}{4} \div \frac{1}{2} = \frac{1}{4} \times \frac{2}{1} = \frac{2}{4} = \frac{1}{2}$$

4 Louise has $4\frac{4}{5}$ yards of red crepe paper. She needs $1\frac{3}{5}$ yards of crepe paper to make a costume for a play. How many costumes can she make?

   Ⓐ $6\frac{1}{5}$ costumes

   Ⓑ 5 costumes

   Ⓒ 4 costumes

   Ⓓ 3 costumes

Step-By-Step

You need to divide $\frac{5}{8}$ by $\frac{1}{16}$ to solve **example 3**. To divide by a fraction, multiply by the reciprocal of the fraction. Review the *Dividing by Fractions* box on this page.

1 Write the reciprocal of $\frac{1}{16}$.

2 Multiply and then simplify the product.

$$\frac{5}{8} \div \frac{1}{16} = \frac{5}{8} \times \frac{16}{1} = \frac{80}{8} = \boxed{}$$

Step-By-Step

To solve **example 4**, you need to divide $4\frac{4}{5}$ by $1\frac{3}{5}$.

1 Write each mixed number as an improper fraction.

$$4\frac{4}{5} = \frac{\boxed{}}{5} \qquad 1\frac{3}{5} = \frac{\boxed{}}{5}$$

2 Write the reciprocal of the divisor, $\frac{8}{5}$, and multiply.

$$\frac{24}{5} \times \frac{5}{8} = \frac{\boxed{}}{\boxed{}}$$

3 Simplify.

GO ON

Dividing Multi-Digit Numbers

5 Ms. Austin is spending 16 nights on vacation at Carr Memorial Suites and Spas. The cost of her stay will be $2,160. What is the cost per night in dollars?

Answer: _____

Remainders

Sometimes, there will be a number left over when you divide. This number is called a *remainder*.

Remainders can be represented using the letter R. They can also be expressed as a fraction or decimal.

$$19 \div 4 = 4\ R3 = 4\tfrac{3}{4} = 4.75$$

Step-By-Step

For **example 5**, you can divide the total cost by the number of nights to find the cost per night.

1 Divide the hundreds.

$$
\begin{array}{r}
1 \\
16\overline{)2160} \\
-\ 16
\end{array}
$$

2 Subtract and bring down the 6 tens. Divide the tens.

$$
\begin{array}{r}
13 \\
16\overline{)2160} \\
-\ 16 \\
\hline
56 \\
-\ 48
\end{array}
$$

3 Subtract and bring down the 0 ones. Divide the ones.

$$
\begin{array}{r}
135 \\
16\overline{)2160} \\
-\ 16 \\
\hline
56 \\
-\ 48 \\
\hline
80 \\
-\ 80 \\
\hline
0
\end{array}
$$

Estimating to Divide

Using Estimation	Increasing an Estimate	Lowering an Estimate
Use rounded numbers. Think: 40 divided into 250 is about 6.	The estimate 4 is too small because the remainder 70 is greater than the divisor 67.	The estimate 8 is too large because you can't subtract 368 from 323.
$$\begin{array}{r} 6 \\ 39\overline{)25,148} \\ -23\ 4 \\ \hline 17 \end{array}$$	$$\begin{array}{r} 4 \\ 67\overline{)33,807} \\ -26\ 8 \\ \hline 70 \end{array}$$	$$\begin{array}{r} 8 \\ 46\overline{)32,374} \\ -36\ 8 \end{array}$$
Multiply 6 × 39 and subtract. Bring down 4 and estimate the next digit.	Increase the estimate to 5.	Lower the estimate to 7.

The Santos family of six and the Purcell family of five vacationed together in Florida.

7   They spent $2,915 for their flight. What was the cost per ticket?

Answer: _____

8   The Santos family's hotel bill was $2,148 for 12 nights. What was the cost per night?

Answer: _____

9   Both families spent $1,980 for meals for 12 days. What was the average cost of food per day per person?

Answer: _____

Adding and Subtracting Decimals

6   George sold his comic book collection. He packed the books in three boxes that weighed 5.25 pounds, 2.3 pounds, and 0.7 pounds. What was the total weight of the boxes?

Ⓐ 5.55 lbs   Ⓒ 7.25 lbs

Ⓑ 6.18 lbs   Ⓓ 8.25 lbs

Remember . . .

When working with decimals, ending zeros can be added or eliminated without changing the value of the number.

2.70 is the same as 2.7.

Step-By-Step

To solve **example 6**, add the weight of the boxes.

1 Write the problem in vertical form and line up the decimal points. It helps to add zeros to the right to make it easier to line up the decimal points.

2 Complete the addition as if the numbers were whole numbers. Bring the decimal straight down into the answer.

$$
\begin{array}{r}
5.25 \\
2.30 \\
+\ 0.70 \\
\hline

\end{array}
$$

 GO ON

Adding and Subtracting Decimals

7 Janelle ran 3.45 miles on Saturday and 4.2 miles on Sunday. How much farther did she run on Sunday?

Ⓐ 0.75 mi

Ⓑ 0.85 mi

Ⓒ 1.25 mi

Ⓓ 1.85 mi

Step-By-Step

Subtract to find "how much farther" in **example 7**.

1 Line up the decimal points to write the problem in vertical form. Add a zero to the right of 4.2 so you can subtract.

$$\begin{array}{r} 4.20 \\ -\ 3.45 \\ \hline \end{array}$$

2 Start at the hundredths place and subtract from right to left.

$$\begin{array}{r} {\scriptstyle 3\ \ 11} \\ {\scriptstyle \cancel{4}\ 10} \\ 4.\cancel{2}0 \\ -\ 3.45 \\ \hline .75 \end{array}$$

Line up the decimal point in the answer with the decimal points in the problem.

Try It

10 Jabar walked 5.5 miles on Monday and 2.75 miles on Tuesday. How much farther did he walk on Monday?

Ⓐ 2.75 mi   Ⓒ 3.25 mi

Ⓑ 2.85 mi   Ⓓ 3.75 mi

11 Manuel sold several video games and his game console. He packed the games in two boxes that weighed 1.7 lbs and 3.3 lbs. He packed the console in a box that weighed 3.25 lbs. What was the total weight of the boxes?

Answer: _____

12 $0.587 - 0.03 =$

Answer: _____

Multiplying and Dividing Decimals

8 The area of a rectangle equals the width times the length. What is the area of a rectangle with a width of 1.08 meters and a length of 2.5 meters?

Ⓐ 2.7 square meters

Ⓑ 3.58 square meters

Ⓒ 4.5 square meters

Ⓓ 45 square meters

Remember . . .

When you multiply decimals, the number of decimal places in the product is the sum of the number of decimal places in the factors.

$$1.003 \longrightarrow \text{3 decimal places}$$
$$\times\, 0.06 \longrightarrow +\,\text{2 decimal places}$$
$$\overline{0.06018 \qquad\quad \text{5 decimal places}}$$

9 A flower bed with a width of 1.2 meters has an area of 4.08 square meters. What is the length of the flower bed?

Ⓐ 34 meters   Ⓒ 3.04 meters

Ⓑ 3.4 meters   Ⓓ 0.34 meter

Remember . . .

When dividing by a decimal, first convert the divisor to a whole number by moving the decimal point. You must move the decimal point in the dividend the same number of places.

$$0.8\overline{)2.\overset{\smile}{8}\overset{\smile}{8}}$$

$$8\overline{)28.8}$$

Step-By-Step

To solve **example 8**, you need to multiply decimals.

1 Write the problem in vertical form. Do NOT line up the decimal points.

2 Multiply as if the numbers were whole numbers. Then count the number of decimal places in the factors. The product must have the same number of decimal places as both factors. Count right to left to place the decimal point.

$$
\begin{array}{r}
1.08 \rightarrow \text{2 decimal places} \\
\times\, 2.5 \rightarrow \text{1 decimal place} \\
\hline
540 \\
+\,2160 \\
\hline
2.700 \leftarrow \text{3 decimal places}
\end{array}
$$

3 Ending zeros in a decimal number can be eliminated without changing the value of the number.

2.700 is the same as 2.7.

Step-By-Step

To solve **example 9**, you will divide a decimal by a decimal.

1 Convert the divisor to a whole number by moving the decimal point. You must move the decimal point in the dividend the same number of places.

$$1.2\overline{)4.08}$$

2 Insert a decimal in the quotient directly above the new decimal in the dividend. Divide as you would with whole numbers. Complete the division.

$$
\begin{array}{r}
3. \\
12\overline{)40.8} \\
-\,36 \\
\hline
\end{array}
$$

13 There are 144 pens in a carton. A factory received an order for 258 cartons. How many pens are in the order? Show your work below.

Answer: _____

14 Area equals length times width. How many square meters are there in the area of a rectangle with dimensions of 0.8 meters and 0.05 meters? Show your work below.

Answer: _____

15 $0.966 \div 14 =$

Ⓐ 0.69   Ⓒ 69

Ⓑ 0.069   Ⓓ 6.9

16 $4.2 \times 0.06 =$

Answer: _____

17 Mr. Ngo has 51.8 meters of fancy braid for a crafts project. Each student needs 1.4 meters. How many students can do the project? Show your work below.

Answer: _____

10 **Part A:** Pedro is selling candy for his school fund-raiser. Chocolate bars cost $1.25 and caramels cost $0.95. If Pedro sells 27 chocolate bars and 35 caramels, how much money does he make for his fund-raiser?

Step 1

27 × ⬚ cost of chocolate bar ⬚ = ⬚

Pedro earned ⬚ by selling chocolate bars.

Step 2

35 × ⬚ cost of caramels ⬚ = ⬚

Pedro earned ⬚ by selling caramels.

Step 3

⬚ money for chocolate bars sold ⬚ + ⬚ money for caramels sold ⬚ = ⬚ total for candy sold ⬚

Pedro earned ⬚ by selling chocolate bars and caramels.

Part B: If the school wants to make $5,025, how many more people would have to sell the same amount as Pedro?

Step 4

5,025 ÷ 67 = _____.

This means that if _____ more people sell $67 worth of candy the school earns its goal amount of $5,025 in its fund-raiser.

Step-By-Step

To solve Part A of this problem, I need to determine how much Pedro sold. Then to solve Part B, I need to divide the total amount of money the school hopes to earn by the amount of money Pedro made for selling both types of candy to see how many people total must sell as much.

Part A

1 First, I'll find how much Pedro earned by selling 27 chocolate bars for $1.25 each.

2 Next, I'll find how much Pedro earned by selling 35 caramels for $0.95 each.

3 I'll add these two totals together to find how much money Pedro made for his fund-raiser.

Part B

4 Now I need to find the total number of people who would have to sell $67 worth of candy for the school to make $5,025. I will divide $5,025 by $67 to determine the total number that would have to sell the same to reach the school goal.

5 Now I need to subtract 1 to find how many more people than Pedro need to sell $67.

GO ON

18 Ahmed wants to save up enough money to buy a new gaming system. The system is $322.50 including tax. He thinks he can save $35 every month from babysitting his neighbor, and his dad promises to give him $5.50 in allowance every month. How many months will he have to save in order to have enough to buy the system? Show your work.

19 Billy and George are competing in a stone-throwing competition. Billy thinks that if he adds his 2 throws together, he will have a distance that is more than twice as far as either one of George's throws. Billy throws a rock 15.6 feet on his first attempt and 17.75 feet on his second attempt. George throws 16.5 feet on his first attempt and 16.1 feet on his second attempt. Was Billy correct? Show your work and explain your reasoning.

20 Gracie wants to buy 6 T-shirts for $4.95 and 2 pairs of pants for $19.95 each. Her mother says she cannot spend more than $75. Will Gracie be able to buy what she wants? If yes, how much money will she have left? If no, how much more money would she need? Show your work.

Go for it!

Test Practice 2: Operations

Directions: Read and answer each question.

1 Divide.

$$0.14\overline{)\$16.80}$$

- Ⓐ $1.20
- Ⓒ $12
- Ⓑ $1.02
- Ⓓ $120

2 $0.478 - 0.03 =$

Answer: _____

3 Divide.

$$76\overline{)6688}$$

Answer: _____

4 What is the perimeter of this polygon?

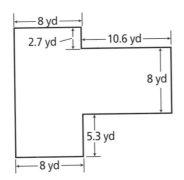

Answer: _____

5 Alexa needs 20.5 pints of blueberries to make jam. She picked 7.75 pints on Friday and 4.25 pints on Saturday. How many more pints does she need to pick?

- Ⓐ 8.5 pints
- Ⓒ 11.5 pints
- Ⓑ 8.25 pints
- Ⓓ 11.75 pints

6 Three families brought 7 pounds of oranges back from vacation in Florida to share. How many pounds of oranges did each family get?

- Ⓐ $2\frac{3}{5}$ pounds
- Ⓒ $3\frac{2}{5}$ pounds
- Ⓑ $2\frac{1}{3}$ pounds
- Ⓓ $3\frac{2}{3}$ pounds

7 Mrs. Sanchez has 30.8 meters of satin trim for blankets. She needs 3.8 meters for each blanket. How many blankets can she make?

Answer: _____

8 A rake is priced at $28.49. Tax is $1.85. What is the total cost of the rake?

Answer: _____

9 Lunch costs $6.90. How much change will Hector get from $20.00?

Answer: _____

10 A garden is 896 square feet in area. It is 32 feet wide. How long is it?

Answer: _____

11 How far does a sailboat travel on a 3.5-hour cruise if its average speed is 18.6 mph?

- Ⓐ 6.51 mi
- Ⓒ 54.1 mi
- Ⓑ 14.88 mi
- Ⓓ 65.1 mi

GO ON

12 Rob has $\frac{15}{16}$ pound of chocolates. He divides it into 5 equal portions. How much does each portion weigh?

   Ⓐ $\frac{5}{16}$ lb   Ⓒ $\frac{3}{16}$ lb

   Ⓑ $\frac{1}{4}$ lb   Ⓓ $\frac{1}{8}$ lb

13 If Mitch rides his bicycle at an average speed of 18 miles per hour, how long will it take him to cover 76.5 miles?

   Ⓐ 1.38 hr   Ⓒ 13.78 hr

   Ⓑ 4.25 hr   Ⓓ 42.5 hr

14 Carla finds that she can make a small pillow from $\frac{3}{8}$ yard of fabric. How many pillows can she make from $4\frac{1}{2}$ yards of fabric?

   Ⓐ $\frac{3}{4}$ Ⓒ 2

   Ⓑ $\frac{4}{3}$ Ⓓ 12

15 A factory worker has 5,500 puzzles to pack into cartons that each hold 785 puzzles. How many puzzles will be left over after the last box is full?

   Ⓐ 5   Ⓒ 7

   Ⓑ 6   Ⓓ 8

16 Mary bought 8 pounds of granola at $3.10 a pound for a family hiking trip. How much did she spend altogether?

   Ⓐ $12.40   Ⓒ $248.00

   Ⓑ $11.10   Ⓓ $24.80

17 Flora is mailing 400 pairs of plastic sunglasses that each weigh 0.08 kg. How much will the entire shipment of sunglasses weigh?

Answer: _____

18 Upper Trail is 6.8 kilometers long. Lower Trail is 7.25 kilometers long. How much longer is Lower Trail?

Answer: _____

19 How many $\frac{1}{4}$-cup servings can Laura make from $\frac{5}{8}$ cup of yogurt?

Answer: _____

20 Mandy is grocery shopping. In her cart are the following items:

5.1 pounds of apples that cost $0.79 a pound

1.9 pounds of beans that cost $1.19 a pound

a can of soup that costs $2.09

a box of cereal that costs $3.59

Mandy has $15. How much will she have after she pays for the groceries?

Show OR describe each step of your work.

Answer: _____

STOP

Number Correct/Total = _____/20

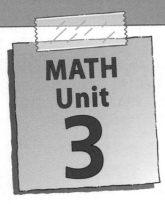

MATH Unit 3

Number Concepts

1 Factors and Multiples [**6.NS.4**]

2 Factors and the Distributive Property [**6.NS.4**]

3 Positive and Negative Numbers [**6.NS.5, 6.NS.6c**]

4 Rational Numbers [**6.NS.6c**]

5 Opposites [**6.NS.6a**]

6 Ordered Pairs [**6.NS.6b, 6.NS6c**]

7 Comparing and Ordering Rational Numbers [**6.NS.7a, 6.NS.7b**]

8 Absolute Value [**6.NS.7c, 6.NS.7d**]

9 Absolute Value and Distance [**6.NS.8**]

Unit 3 Application [**6.NS.5, 6.NS.6a, 6.NS.6b, 6.NS.6c, 6.NS.8**]

Directions: Read and answer each question.

Factors and Multiples

1 A coach is dividing 24 girls and 40 boys into teams. Each team must have the same number of members, and each team must have either all boys or all girls. What is the greatest number of members that can be on a team?

Ⓐ 4

Ⓑ 8

Ⓒ 12

Ⓓ 24

Factors

A **factor** is a number that divides evenly into another number. The **greatest common factor (GCF)** is the largest factor that is common to two or more numbers.

Factors of 8: 1, 2, ④, 8

Factors of 12: 1, 2, 3, ④, 6, 12

The GCF of 8 and 12 is 4.

Step-By-Step

To solve **example 1**, find the greatest common factor of 24 and 40. This is the greatest number that can divide evenly into both numbers.

1 List the factors of 24.

Factors of 24: 1, 2, 3, 4, 6, 8, 12, 24

2 List the factors of 40.

Factors of 40: 1, 2, 4, 5, 8, 10, 20, 40

3 What is the greatest common factor of 24 and 40?

Factors and Multiples

2 Starting today, Hal will clean his room every 6 days. Vance will clean his room every 8 days. How long will it be until the first time they clean their rooms on the same day?

Ⓐ 16 days   Ⓒ 32 days

Ⓑ 24 days   Ⓓ 48 days

Remember . . .

To find **multiples** of a number, multiply the number by whole numbers.

Multiples of 3:

3	6	9	12, etc.
3×1	3×2	3×3	3×4

Factors and the Distributive Property

3 Which expression is equivalent to $42 + 18$?

Ⓐ $4(9 + 4)$

Ⓑ $7(6 + 2)$

Ⓒ $3(12 + 6)$

Ⓓ $6(7 + 3)$

The Distributive Property

The **distributive property** lets you multiply each number in a sum and then add the products.

$5(3 + 4) = (5 \times 3) + (5 \times 4)$
$= 15 + 20$
$= 35$

The distributive property lets you break sums into parts by separating out common factors.

$15 + 20 = (5 \times 3) + (5 \times 4) = 5(3 + 4)$

Step-By-Step

Example 2 asks you to find the **least common multiple** of 6 and 8. This is the least number into which both numbers will divide evenly.

1 List the first five multiples of 6.

Multiples of 6: 6, 12, 18, 24, 30, . . .

2 List the first five multiples of 8.

Multiples of 8: 8, 16, 24, 32, 40, . . .

3 What is the least common multiple of 6 and 8?

Step-By-Step

For **example 3**, 42 and 18 have a common factor. Use the **distributive property** to rewrite the expression as the sum of two numbers with no common factor.

1 Find factors for 42 and 18.

Factors of 42: 1, 2, 3, 6, 7, 14, 28, 42

Factors of 18: 1, 2, 3, 6, 9, 18

2 Choose the **greatest common factor (GCF)**. Write 42 and 18 as products with the GCF as one factor.

$42 + 18 = (\boxed{} \times 7) + (\boxed{} \times 3)$

3 Use the distributive property to simplify the expression.

$(6 \times 7) + (6 \times 3) = \boxed{} (7 + 3)$

1 What is the greatest common factor of 12 and 20? Factor the numbers and show your work below.

Answer: _____

2 Which numbers have 4 as a common factor?

Ⓐ 2, 6   Ⓒ 9, 12

Ⓑ 8, 12   Ⓓ 10, 12

3 What common factor can be used to reduce $\frac{24}{30}$ to the lowest terms?

Ⓐ 3   Ⓒ 6

Ⓑ 4   Ⓓ 8

4 Write the greatest common factor of 18 and 28.

Answer: _____

5 What is the least common multiple of 10 and 12?

Answer: _____

6 Choose the least common multiple of 6 and 9.

Ⓐ 12   Ⓒ 27

Ⓑ 18   Ⓓ 54

7 Which expression is equal to 54 + 48?

Ⓐ 12(5 + 4)

Ⓑ 6(9 + 8)

Ⓒ 9(6 + 8)

Ⓓ 8(9 + 6)

GO ON

4 Katie drew this picture to show the elevations of her favorite rock and her favorite dive spot.

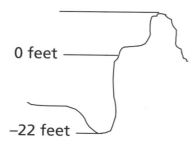

0 feet

−22 feet

Her favorite dive spot is below sea level, so she labeled it −22 feet. Sea level is 0 feet. Katie's favorite rock is 10 feet above sea level. What number should she use to label it?

Answer: _____

Positive and Negative Numbers

Numbers less than zero are **negative numbers.** A negative sign (−) before a number shows a negative number:

$$-18 \quad -\tfrac{3}{5} \quad -6.73$$

Numbers greater than zero are **positive numbers**. A positive sign (+) before a number shows a positive number.

$$+24 \quad +\tfrac{3}{5} \quad +0.02$$

If a number does not have a sign, it is a positive number.

Think It Through

For **example 4**, 0 shows sea level. The negative number −22 shows distance below sea level. Write a positive number to show that the rock is 10 feet above sea level.

+ ☐

5 Which point on the number line is located at 1.5?

A B   C D

$$\begin{array}{ccccccc} -3 & -2 & -1 & 0 & 1 & 2 & 3 \end{array}$$

Ⓐ point A

Ⓑ point B

Ⓒ point C

Ⓓ point D

Rational Numbers

A **rational number** is any number that can be written as the ratio of two integers.

The fractions $\frac{1}{2}$ and $-\frac{3}{4}$ and the decimals 0.5 and -0.75 are examples of rational numbers.

Step-By-Step

To solve **example 5**, you must locate the **rational number** 1.5 on a number line.

1 Points to the right of zero are positive rational numbers. Points to the left of zero are negative rational numbers. You are trying to locate a positive rational number. Which points can you eliminate?

☐ and ☐

2 To locate 1.5, find the point that is between 1 and 2.

Try It

8 Mark the following numbers on the number line below. Circle the positive rational numbers.

$$6.5 \quad -5 \quad -8.5 \quad 8$$

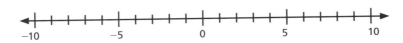

$$\begin{array}{cccc} -10 & -5 & 0 & 5 & 10 \end{array}$$

GO ON

Use this number line for examples 6 and 7.

6 What is the opposite of +6?

Answer: _____

7 What is the opposite of the opposite of +6?

Answer: _____

Opposites

Numbers that are the same distance from zero but on opposite sides of zero on a number line are **opposites**.

The opposite of 3.68 is −3.68.

The opposite of $-\frac{7}{10}$ is $\frac{7}{10}$.

The opposite of 0 is 0.

Think It Through

For **example 6**, +6 is 6 units to the right of zero. The number 6 units to the left of zero is its opposite.

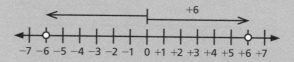

Step-By-Step

For **example 7**, first find the opposite of +6, then find the opposite of that number.

1 What is the opposite of +6? ☐

2 What is the opposite of −6? ☐

3 What is the opposite of the opposite of +6? ☐

Ordered Pairs

8 In what quadrant is point $(-2, -5)$ located?

    Ⓐ Quadrant I

    Ⓑ Quadrant II

    Ⓒ Quadrant III

    Ⓓ Quadrant IV

The Coordinate Grid

The **axes** of the **coordinate grid** are horizontal and vertical number lines that meet at their zero points. This meeting point is called the *origin* and is $(0, 0)$ on the coordinate grid.

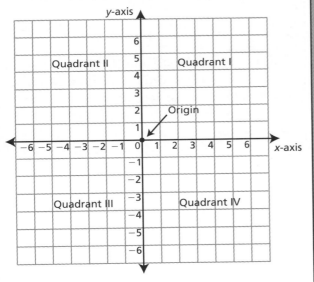

The horizontal number line is the *x*-axis. The vertical number line is the *y*-axis. The number lines divide the coordinate grid into four quadrants.

Locations on the grid are given using an **ordered pair** of numbers (*x*-coordinate, *y*-coordinate) that tells the distance from $(0, 0)$. The first number tells the horizontal distance right $(+)$ or left $(-)$. The second tells the vertical distance up $(+)$ or down $(-)$.

Step-By-Step

Locate the point for **example 8**. Then look at *The Coordinate Grid* box to identify the quadrant.

1 Start at $(0, 0)$. The *x*-coordinate for the ordered pair is –2. The negative sign tells you to move 2 units left along the *x*-axis. The *y*-coordinate is –5. The negative sign tells you to move down 5 units.

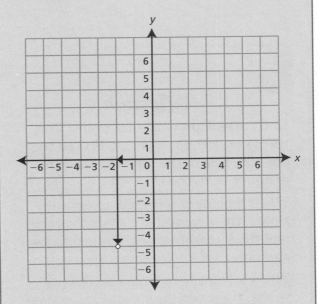

2 The numbers for the quadrants are shown in *The Coordinate Grid* box. In what quadrant is point $(-2, -5)$ located?

Ordered Pairs

9 If point (−4, 3) is reflected across the horizontal *x*-axis, what are the coordinates of the point?

Answer: _____

Reflection

In a **reflection** of a point over a line, the point is flipped so that it is on the opposite side of the line and the same distance from the line.

When a point is reflected across the *x*-axis, the *x*-coordinate stays the same and the *y*-coordinate is changed to its opposite.

When a point is reflected across the *y*-axis, the *y*-coordinate stays the same and the *x*-coordinate is changed to its opposite.

Think It Through

Locate point (−4 , 3) on the coordinate grid. Then find the point that is the same distance from the *x*-axis, but on the opposite side.

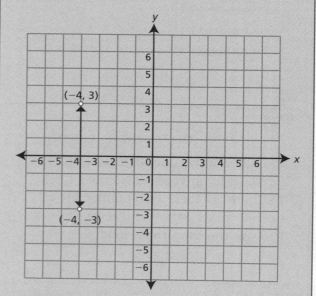

The *x*-coordinate of the reflection is the same as the *x*-coordinate of the original point. The *y*-coordinate of the reflection is the opposite of the *y*-coordinate of the original point.

Ordered Pairs

10 Which statement is NOT true about these ordered pairs?

$(-4, 3), (-4, -3), (4, 3), (4, -3)$

Ⓐ Their points are reflections over the axes.

Ⓑ Each orderd pair is located in a different quadrant.

Ⓒ Their coordinates are the same except for signs.

Ⓓ The horizontal and vertical distances from $(0, 0)$ are all different.

Try It

9 Name the coordinates of each point on the grid.

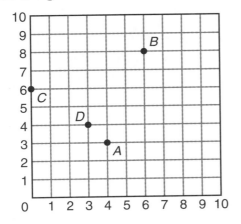

Point A _____

Point B _____

Point C _____

Point D _____

Step-By-Step

For **example 10**, graph the 4 points and then use the coordinates and the points to check each statement.

1 Graph each point.

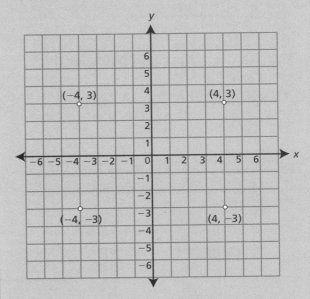

2 Write *True* or *False* for each statement. Choose the statement that is NOT true.

The points are reflections over the axes. _____

Each point is in a different quadrant. _____

The coordinates are the same except for signs. _____

The horizontal and vertical distances from $(0, 0)$ are all different. _____

GO ON

Try It *continued*

10 What is located at (1, 4)?

Ⓐ Middle School
Ⓑ Park
Ⓒ Public Library
Ⓓ Science Museum

11 What are the coordinates for the Park?

Ⓐ (0, 2)   Ⓒ (2, 2)
Ⓑ (2, 0)   Ⓓ (2, 3)

12 Which point is halfway between the Middle School and the Shopping Mall?

Ⓐ (2, 2)   Ⓒ (4, 4)
Ⓑ (3, 3)   Ⓓ (4, 2)

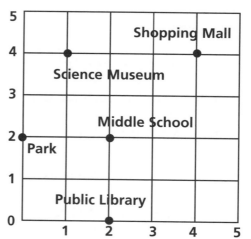

Comparing and Ordering Rational Numbers

11 Marcos keeps track of the daily high temperatures in his town. He made this chart during a recent cold snap.

Day	High Temperature (°F)
Mon.	−7°
Tues.	−4°
Wed.	−11°
Thurs.	−3°

On which day was the high temperature the warmest?

Ⓐ Monday
Ⓑ Tuesday
Ⓒ Wednesday
Ⓓ Thursday

Step-By-Step

For **example 11**, the warmest temperature is the number farthest right on a number line.

1 Graph the integers on a number line to compare them.

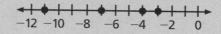

2 As you move from left to right, the integers go from lesser to greater. Which number did you graph the farthest to the right?

Comparing and Ordering Rational Numbers

12 Which statement is true?

Ⓐ $-2 > -1$

Ⓑ $1\frac{1}{2} < 1\frac{1}{4}$

Ⓒ $-1\frac{1}{2} < 1$

Ⓓ $-\frac{3}{4} > -\frac{1}{4}$

Inequality Symbols

$<$ means *is less than*.

$>$ means *is greater than*.

Think It Through

You can use a number line to compare the numbers in **example 12**.

Choice Ⓐ states that -2 is greater than -1. Graph these numbers on a number line. Is -2 greater than -1?

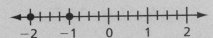

Evaluate the other answers by graphing the numbers on the number line.

Which answer shows a true statement?

Try It

Add $<$ or $>$. To evaluate each, graph each pair of choices on a number line.

13 $-2 \ \square \ 2$

14 $\frac{1}{2} \ \square \ -1\frac{1}{2}$

15 $-8 \ \square \ -3$

16 $6 \ \square \ -8$

GO ON

Absolute Value

13 What is $|-4|$?

Answer: _____

Absolute Value

The absolute value of a number is its distance from 0 on a number line. Absolute value tells how far, so it is always positive.

Positive 6 is 6 units to the right of zero, so its absolute value is 6: $|6| = 6$

Negative 6 is 6 units to the left of zero, so its absolute value is 6: $|-6| = 6$

14 The temperature is $-12°$. How many degrees below zero is the temperature?

Answer: _____

15 Ben's score for a computer game is -3600. Which statement is true about his score?

Ⓐ The score is less than 3000 points below zero.

Ⓑ The score is more than 3000 points below zero.

Ⓒ The score is 3000 points above zero.

Ⓓ The score is more than 3000 points above zero.

Step-By-Step

Example 13 is read "What is the absolute value of –4?"

1 Graph –4.

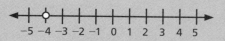

2 The absolute value is the distance –4 is from 0.

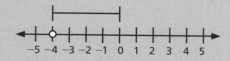

What number tells how far it is from 0 to –4? ☐

Think It Through

For **example 14**, the number of degrees below zero is the absolute value of the temperature.

$$|-12| = \boxed{}$$

Step-By-Step

In **example 15**, the negative sign in –3600 shows that the score is less than 0.

1 –3600 is below zero. Which answer choices can be eliminated?

Eliminate: ☐ and ☐

2 3000 points below zero is –3000. Think of a number line.

Is –3600 closer or farther from zero than –3000? _____

3 Choose the answer that says –3600 is farther from zero than –3000.

Absolute Value and Distance

This coordinate grid shows Nora's school, the library, Nora's house, and Antonio's house. Each square is 1 block. Use the grid for **examples 16** and **17**.

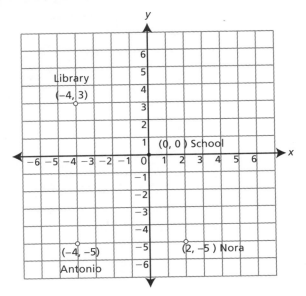

16 How far is it from Nora's house to Antonio's house?

Answer: _____ blocks

17 How many blocks is it from Antonio's house to the library?

Answer: _____ blocks

Step-By-Step

For **example 16**, you need to find the distance between points $(2, -5)$ and $(-4, -5)$.

1 $(2, -5)$ and $(-4, -5)$ have the same y-coordinate, so you can find the distance between them by adding the absolute values of the x-coordinates. Find the absolute value of each x-coordinate.

$|2| = $ ☐

$|-4| = $ ☐

2 Add the absolute values.

$2 + 4 = $ ☐

Step-By-Step

For **example 17**, you need to find the distance between points $(-4, -5)$ and $(-4, 3)$.

1 $(-4, -5)$ and $(-4, 3)$ have the same x-coordinate, so you can find the distance between them by adding the absolute values of the y-coordinates. Find the absolute value of each y-coordinate.

$|-5| = $ ☐

$|3| = $ ☐

2 Add the absolute values.

$5 + 3 = $ ☐

GO ON

18 Juan and Alisha are running errands in town. They are going to the Theatre, Pizza Parlor, Grocery Store, Post Office, and Bank. Each destination is given below with its coordinates. Graph each location and label it. Then state the total distance of their trip. Juan and Alisha must stay on the lines and cannot go diagonally. They will always take the shortest route. Each square is one block.

Stop 1: Theatre (6, 2)

Stop 2: Pizza Parlor (3, 5)

Stop 3: Grocery Story (−2, 5)

Stop 4: Post Office (−2, −3)

Stop 5: Bank (6, −3)

Return to Theatre to go home.

Step-By-Step

1 First I will plot and label the locations where Juan and Alisha stopped. I'll write the coordinates next to the locations. Then I will total the distances by comparing the coordinates.

2 I can find the distance between the Theatre and the Pizza Parlor by comparing the values of the points. The Theatre is at (6, 2) and the Pizza Parlor is at (3, 5).

Step 1

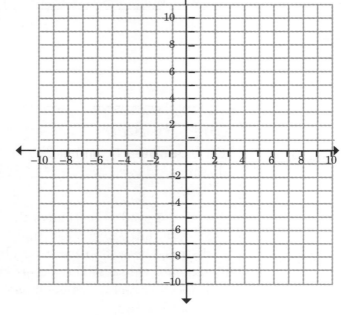

Step 2

I'll look at the *x*-values first.

6 is [ ] bigger than 3. So, Juan and Alisha walk

[ ] blocks left.

Then I compare the *y*-values. 5 is [ ] blocks more than 2.

So the Pizza Parlor is [ ] blocks away. I can check by counting over and up

from the Theatre to the Pizza Parlor.

Step 3

The Pizza Parlor is at (3, 5) and the Grocery is at (–2, 5).

2 + 3 = ☐ .

Juan and Alisha walk ☐ blocks from the Pizza Parlor to the Grocery.

Step 4

Juan and Alisha walk ☐ blocks from the Grocery to the Post Office.

Step 5

Juan and Alisha walk ☐ blocks from the Post Office to the Bank.

To return to the Theatre, the two walk ☐ blocks from the Bank.

Step 6

☐ + ☐ + ☐ + ☐ +

☐ = ☐

Juan and Alisha walked ☐ blocks on their errands.

Step-By-Step

3 To determine the distance from the Pizza Parlor to the Grocery, I compare the x-coordinates because the y-coordinates are the same. I count left from 3 to 0, which equals 3, and from 0 to –2, which equals 2.

4 For the next part of their journey, I will compare the coordinates for the Grocery and the Post Office. Since the x-values are the same, I evaluate the absolute value of both y-values to determine the distance.

5 For the last errand, the two walk from the Post Office to the Bank. Since the y-coordinates are the same, I compare the x-values. Then I can finish the journey by taking the two back to the Theatre.

6 Finally, I add all the distances together.

GO ON

17 Bill is planting flowers in his yard. Each flower sits at a corner of the garden. Find the distance around the garden. Each block represents 1 foot. Plot the location of each flower and then determine the total distance around the garden. Show all your work.

Flower 1: (1, 3)

Flower 2: (2, 3)

Flower 3: (2, –4)

Flower 4: (–3, –4)

Flower 5: (–3, –3)

Flower 6: (1, –3)

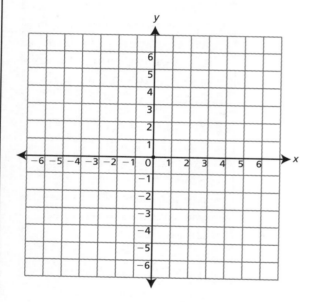

Answer: _____

_____

_____

_____

_____

18 Johanna is training for a half marathon. If she runs between 3 parks, can she get in her required 10 training miles today, assuming she returns to the original park? The centers of each park are given. She must stay on the grid and will always take the shortest path. Plot her route and find the total distance she ran and whether she got in her 10 training miles. Each square is one mile. Show all your work.

Park 1: (2, 2)

Park 2: (–2, 1)

Park 3: (0, 0)

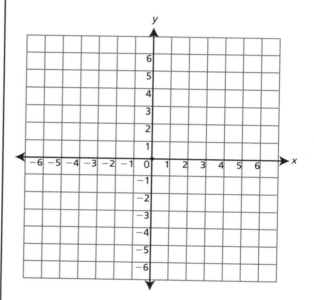

Answer: _____

_____

_____

_____

_____

Go for it!

Test Practice 3: Number Concepts

Directions: Read and answer each question.

1 What is the least common multiple of 4 and 18?

Ⓐ 2   Ⓒ 36

Ⓑ 12   Ⓓ 72

2 What is the greatest common factor of 24 and 36?

Ⓐ 2   Ⓒ 12

Ⓑ 6   Ⓓ 72

3 Which expression is equal to 72 + 63?

Ⓐ 9 (8 + 7)

Ⓑ 8 (9 + 7)

Ⓒ 7 (10 + 9)

Ⓓ 6 (12 + 10)

4 What number shows a temperature of 9° below zero?

Answer: _____

5 Emma's house is 492 feet above sea level. What number can be used to represent sea level?

Answer: _____

6 Which integer is less than −2?

Ⓐ −6   Ⓒ 2

Ⓑ 0   Ⓓ 6

7 Tanya is building a tower with blocks that are 3 inches high. Val is building a tower with blocks that are 7 inches high. What is the shortest tower each can build if they want their towers to be the same height?

Answer: _____

8 What number is represented by point A on the number line?

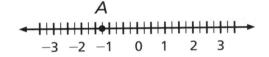

Ⓐ $-\frac{3}{4}$ Ⓒ $-\frac{5}{4}$

Ⓑ -1.5 Ⓓ -1.75

9 What is the absolute value of 8?

Answer: _____

10 Pat is making flower bouquets. She has 12 roses, 21 daisies, and 45 carnations. All of the bouquets must be exactly alike. What is the greatest number of bouquets that Pat can make if she uses all the flowers? Explain how you got your answer.

Answer: _____

Explanation: _____

_____

_____

_____

_____

GO ON

11 Which letter shows the opposite of −5?

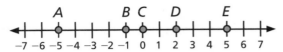

Answer: _____

12 What number is the opposite of 6.2?

Answer: _____

13 What number is the opposite of the opposite of −15?

Answer: _____

14 Which statement is true?

  Ⓐ $-5 > -3$ Ⓒ $-\frac{7}{8} < -\frac{3}{4}$

  Ⓑ $1\frac{2}{3} < -1\frac{4}{5}$ Ⓓ $1 > \frac{10}{7}$

15 A point has a negative *x*-value and a positive *y*-value.

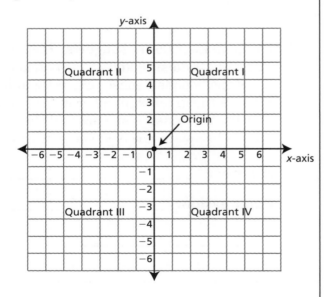

In what quadrant is it located?

  Ⓐ Quadrant I   Ⓒ Quadrant III

  Ⓑ Quadrant II   Ⓓ Quadrant IV

16 A point is reflected over the *y*-axis. The coordinates of the reflection are (−5, 6). What are the coordinates of the original point?

Answer: _____

17 Which statement is true about two ordered pairs that are the same except for the signs of the numbers?

  Ⓐ Their points are reflections.

  Ⓑ Their points are on the horizontal axis.

  Ⓒ Their points are on the vertical axis.

  Ⓓ Their points are in different quadrants.

18 Which point on the number line is located at 4?

  Ⓐ point *A*   Ⓒ point *C*

  Ⓑ point *B*   Ⓓ point *D*

19 Which is the best estimate of the location of point *P*?

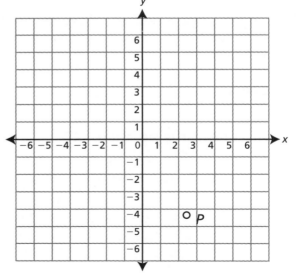

  Ⓐ $(-4.2, 2.5)$ Ⓒ $(2.5, -4.2)$

  Ⓑ $(-2.2, 4.5)$ Ⓓ $(4.5, -3.2)$

20 What are the coordinates of the reflection of $(5, -2)$ over the *x*-axis?

Answer: _____

21 Ben's bank balance is $-\$14$. How many dollars below zero is his bank balance?

Answer: _____

22 Use the distributive property to write $35 + 50$ as a sum of two numbers with no common factors.

Answer: _____

23 Use this grid to show the locations of the benches in Lincoln Park.

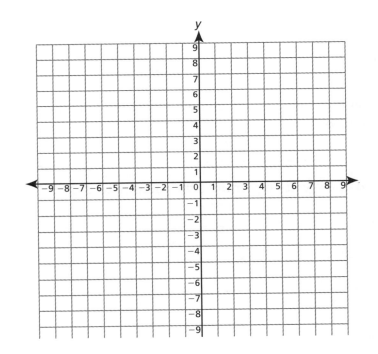

Bench A: (5, 7)
Bench B: (1, 3)
Bench C: (–7, 3)
Bench D: (–7, –6)
Bench E: (5, –6)

Each square shows 1 meter.

A What is the distance between Bench A and Bench E?

Answer: _____

B What is the distance between Bench B and Bench C?

Answer: _____

GO ON

24   Cabrini charted the noon temperatures in six cities on her birthday, January 27.

City	Temperature °F
Belford	3°
Fern	−12°
Ableton	10°
Caraway	−3°
Verdant	−8°
Valley Lo	6°

Part A

Write the temperatures in order from least to greatest.

Answer: _____

Part B

Which city's noon temperature was greater than the temperature in Verdant, but less than the temperature in Belford?

Answer: _____

Explain in words how you determined the answer to Part B.

Explanation: _____

_____

_____

_____

_____

Number Correct/Total = _____/24

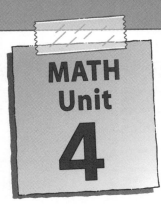

MATH Unit 4

Expressions

1 Exponents [6.EE.1]
2 Writing Expressions [6.EE.2a, 6.EE.2b]
3 Evaluating Expressions [6.EE.2c]
4 Using Formulas [6.EE.2c]
5 Equivalent Expressions [6.EE.3, 6.EE.4]
Unit 4 Application [6.EE.2a, 6.EE.2b, 6.EE.2c, 6.EE.4]

Directions: Read and answer each question.

Exponents

1 What is the exponential form for
$7 \times 7 \times 7 \times 7 \times 7$?

  ⓐ 5^7 ⓒ 7^5

  ⓑ 7^3 ⓓ 7^7

Remember . . .

Exponential Form	Factor Form	Standard Form
↓	↓	↓

$$10^3 = 10 \times 10 \times 10 = 1,000$$

Base Exponent

2 What is the standard form of this expression?

$$2^4$$

  ⓐ 16   ⓒ 32

  ⓑ 24   ⓓ 64

Step-By-Step

Example 1 asks you to change an expression written in factor form into an expression with an exponent. An **exponent** shows how many times the base is used as a factor.

1 Identify the base. The base is the factor that is repeated.

    The base is ____ .

2 Count the number of times the factor is repeated. This is the exponent.

$$7 \times 7 \times 7 \times 7 \times 7 = 7^{\boxed{}}$$

Step-By-Step

To solve **example 2**, you must find the value of an expression written in exponent form.

1 Write 2^4 in factor form by multiplying four 2s together.

$$2^4 = \boxed{}$$

2 Find the product.

$$2 \times 2 \times 2 \times 2 = \boxed{}$$

GO ON ➡

Writing Expressions

3 Which expression represents *8 more than 3 times a number*?

   Ⓐ $3n - 8$ Ⓒ $3 + 8n$

   Ⓑ $8 + 3n$ Ⓓ $8 + n + 3$

Remember . . .

A number followed by a variable shows multiplication: $2m = 2 \times m$.

A fraction bar shows division: $\frac{p}{3} = p \div 3$.

4 A number is added to 2. The sum is then multiplied by 5. Which expression represents this situation?

   Ⓐ $2n + 5$ Ⓒ $2(n + 5)$

   Ⓑ $5n + 2$ Ⓓ $5(n + 2)$

Variables

Variables are letters that stand for unknown numbers in expressions or equations.

5 The cost to go bowling is $7 per game (*g*) plus $6 to rent a pair of shoes. Which mathematical expression can be used to show the cost to go bowling?

   Ⓐ $g \times \$6 + \$7$

   Ⓑ $g \times (\$7 + \$6)$

   Ⓒ $g \div (\$6 + \$7)$

   Ⓓ $g \times \$7 + \$6$

Think It Through

Remember, an algebraic expression does NOT contain an $=$. In **example 3**, let *n* stand for the unknown number.

Replace *more than* with a plus sign and *number* with *n*.

8 <u>more than</u> 3 times a <u>number</u>

$8 + 3$ ☐

Step-By-Step

In **example 4**, notice that the addition is done before the multiplication.

1 Use the letter *n* as the variable and add 2 to it.

$$n + 2$$

2 The statement says that the sum is multiplied by 5. You will need to put parentheses around $n + 2$ to indicate that the addition goes first.

$$(n + 2) \times 5$$

3 Which answer choice is similar to the above expression?

In **example 5**, the variable *g* represents the number of games bowled.

1 It costs $7 to bowl one game. Write an expression to find the cost of bowling *g* games.

$$g \times \text{☐}$$

2 There is also a $6 shoe rental fee. This fee does not vary with the number of games bowled. Add this fee to the expression to find the total cost.

$$g \times \$7 + \text{☐}$$

6 What are the terms of the expression $-4x + 8$?

    Ⓐ -4 and x Ⓒ -4 and 8

    Ⓑ 4 and 8 Ⓓ $-4x$ and 8

Think It Through

For **example 6**, refer to the *Terms of an Expression* box. What are the two parts of the expression that are connected by a + or − sign?

Terms of an Expression

The **terms** in an algebraic expression are the parts of the expression connected by + or − signs.

The **coefficient** of a term is a number that is multiplied by a variable.

$8y$ is a single-term expression with coefficient 8. Its factors are 8 and y.

A **constant** term is a number that does not have a variable factor.

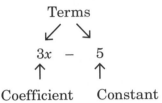

Try It

1 What is the exponential form for $6 \times 6 \times 6 \times 6 \times 6$?

Answer: _____

2 What is the standard form for 5^3?

    Ⓐ 125   Ⓒ 25

    Ⓑ 53   Ⓓ 15

3 Choose the expression that represents this phrase.

    16 less than a number

    Ⓐ $n - 16$ Ⓒ $16 - n$

    Ⓑ $n \div 16$ Ⓓ $n + 16$

Write an expression for the phrase. Use *n* for the unknown number.

4 *a number decreased by 5*

    Answer: _____

5 *a number decreased by 6*

    Answer: _____

6 *12 more than a number*

    Answer: _____

7 *4 less than twice a number*

    Answer: _____

8 What is the coefficient of x in the following expression?

    $4x + 8$

    Answer: _____

GO ON

Evaluating Expressions

7 What is the value of $2w - 6$ when $w = 10$?

Ⓐ 16   Ⓒ 4

Ⓑ 14   Ⓓ 2

Order of Operations

Step 1: Do calculations within grouping symbols (parentheses).

Step 2: Evaluate exponents.

Step 3: Multiply and divide from left to right.

Step 4: Add and subtract from left to right.

8 Simplify this expression for $x = 7$ and $y = 3$.

$$(y + 3x) \div 4 + x^2 - 36$$

Answer: _____

Step-By-Step

In **example 7**, the expression is $2w - 6$. You are asked to **evaluate** the expression when the variable w has the value 10.

1 Substitute 10 for the variable w.

$$(2 \times \boxed{}) - 6$$

2 The expression is now a numerical expression. Evaluate by multiplying and then subtracting.

$$(2 \times 10) - 6$$

$$20 - 6 = \boxed{}$$

Step-By-Step

1 First, substitute 7 for x and 3 for y.

$$(y + 3x) \div 4 + x^2 - 36$$

$$(3 + 3 \times 7) \div 4 + (7)^2 - 36$$

2 Simplify the parentheses first. Then simplify the exponent.

$$(3 + 21) \div 4 + (7)^2 - 36$$

$$24 \div 4 + \boxed{} - 36$$

3 Divide.

$$24 \div 4 + 49 - 36$$

$$6 + 49 - 36$$

4 Add and subtract from left to right.

$$6 + 49 - 36$$

$$\boxed{} - 36$$

$$\boxed{}$$

9 What is the value of $20 - 3k$ when $k = 4$?

Answer: _____

10 For which value of d is $\frac{d}{3}$ equal to 6?

ⓐ $\frac{1}{3}$ ⓒ 2

ⓑ $\frac{1}{2}$ ⓓ 18

11 Gail is 6 years younger than Mark. Let m = Mark's age. Which expression equals Gail's age?

ⓐ $6m$ ⓒ $m - 6$

ⓑ $m + 6$ ⓓ $6 - m$

12 If $a = 10$, $b = 1$, and $c = 5$, what is the value of $ab + bc$? Show your work below.

Answer: _____

Using Formulas

9 Nora built an end table that is in the shape of a cube. To decide how much paint to buy, she needs to find its surface area. Each side of the cube is 16 inches. Use the formula $SA = 6s^2$. What is the surface area of the table?

Answer: _____

Step-By-Step

For **example 9**, substitute 16 for s in the formula. Then evaluate the expression to find the area of the cube.

1 Substitute 16 for s.

$SA = 6s^2$

$SA = 6(16^2)$

2 Use the order of operations to evaluate the expression. First evaluate 16^2. Then multiply.

$SA = 6(\underline{\hspace{1cm}})$

$SA = \underline{\hspace{1cm}}$

GO ON

Using Formulas

10 Marcos walked his dog around the outside of the dog park. The park is a rectangle 88.5 meters long and 56.2 meters wide. What is the perimeter of the park? Use the formula $P = 2l + 2w$.

Answer: _____

Step-By-Step

For **example 10**, substitute values for length and width into the formula. Then use the order of operations to calculate the perimeter.

1 Substitute 88.5 for l and 56.2 for w in the perimeter formula.

$$P = 2l + 2w$$

$$P = 2(88.5) + 2(\underline{\quad\quad})$$

2 Multiply.

$$P = \underline{\quad\quad} + \underline{\quad\quad}$$

3 Add.

$$P = 177 + 112.4 = \underline{\quad\quad}$$

Try It

13 Use the formula $P = 2l + 2w$. Find the perimeter of a carpet that is 3 yards long and 4 feet wide.

Answer: _____

14 Use the formula $A = \frac{1}{2} \times bh$. The area of a small triangular garden is 40 square yards. The height is 10 yards. Find the base.

Answer: _____

15 David used 40 feet of braid to trim the edges of a quilt that is 12 feet long. How wide is the quilt? Use the formula $P = 2l + 2w$.

Ⓒ $3\frac{1}{3}$ ft   Ⓔ 14 ft

Ⓓ 8 ft   Ⓕ 28 ft

16 Use the formula $A = \frac{1}{2} \times bh$. In a right triangle, the base is n units and the height is 3 times that long. Write a formula for the area of this triangle.

Answer: _____

Equivalent Expressions

11 Simplify this expression.

$$7x + 5x$$

Answer: _____

Step-By-Step

To simplify an algebraic expression, write it in the most compact way. This usually involves *combining like terms*.

1 You can use the distributive property to combine like terms. Factor out the common factor, x, in each term.

$$7x + 5x$$

$$(7 + 5)x$$

2 Add the numbers in the parentheses.

$$(7 + 5)x = \boxed{}\,x$$

Properties of Operations

Property	Definition	Example
Identity Property of Addition	The sum of any number and 0 is the original number.	$x + 0 = x$
Identity Property of Multiplication	The product of any number and 1 is the original number.	$y \times 1 = y$
Distributive Property	The product of a number and a sum or difference is the same as the sum or difference of each product taken separately.	$x(y + z) = xy + xz$ $a(b - c) = ab - ac$
Associative Property	Addends and factors can be regrouped without affecting the answer.	$x + (y + z) = (x + y) + z$ $a \times (b \times c) = (a \times b) \times c$
Commutative Property	The order in which numbers are added or multiplied does not affect the answer.	$x + y = y + x$ $a \times b = b \times a$

Ordered Pairs

8 In what quadrant is point $(-2, -5)$ located?

Ⓒ Quadrant I
Ⓓ Quadrant II
Ⓔ Quadrant III
Ⓕ Quadrant IV

The Coordinate Grid

The **axes** of the **coordinate grid** are horizontal and vertical number lines that meet at their zero points. This meeting point is called the *origin* and is $(0, 0)$ on the coordinate grid.

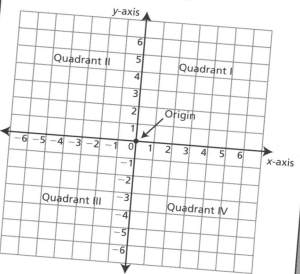

The horizontal number line is the x-axis. The vertical number line is the y-axis. The number lines divide the coordinate grid into four quadrants.

Locations on the grid are given using an **ordered pair** of numbers (x-coordinate, y-coordinate) that tells the distance from $(0, 0)$. The first number tells the horizontal dista...

Step-By-Step

Locate the point for **example 8**. Then look at *The Coordinate Grid* box to identify the quadrant.

1 Start at $(0, 0)$. The x-coordinate for the ordered pair is -2. The negative sign tells you to move 2 units left along the x-axis. The y-coordinate is -5. The negative sign tells you to move down 5 units.

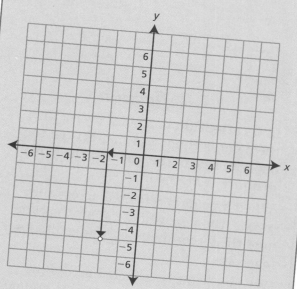

2 The numbers for the quadrants are shown in *The Coordinate Grid* box. In what quadrant is point $(-2, -5)$ located?

Equivalent Expressions

12 Which expression is equivalent to $15 + n + 6$?

  Ⓐ $9n$

  Ⓑ $21n$

  Ⓒ $9 + n$

  Ⓓ $21 + n$

Remember . . .

If two expressions are equivalent, both will have the same value no matter what number is substituted for the variable.

13 Which expression is equivalent to $21m + 28n$?

  Ⓐ $49(m + n)$

  Ⓑ $49mn$

  Ⓒ $7(3m + 4n)$

  Ⓓ $21(m + 7n)$

Step-By-Step

For **example 12**, use the Commutative Property to rearrange the terms.

1 Rearrange the terms so they are easier to add.

$$15 + 6 + \boxed{}$$

2 Simplify.

$$\boxed{} + n$$

Step-By-Step

For **example 13**, use the distributive property to separate out common factors.

1 Find the greatest common factor for 21 and 28.

Factors of 21: 1, 3, 7, 21

Factors of 28: 1, 2, 4, 7, 14, 28

The greatest common factor is $\boxed{}$

2 Factor 7 out of each term.

$$21m + 28n = 7(\boxed{}\,m) + 7(\boxed{}\,n)$$

3 Simplify the expression.

$$7(3m) + 7(4n) = \boxed{}\,(3m + 4n)$$

Try It

17 Simplify this expression.

$$5y + 3y$$

Answer: _____

18 Which expression is equivalent to $3n + 5 - 6$?

  Ⓐ $3n + 11$ Ⓒ $3n - 1$

  Ⓑ $8n - 6$ Ⓓ $3n + 1$

19 Which expression is equivalent to $28x + 49y$?

  Ⓐ $77(x + y)$ Ⓒ $77 + y$

  Ⓑ $7(4x + 7y)$ Ⓓ $21(7x + 28y)$

---

the horizontal x and y, coordinates of the point?

Answer: _____

Reflection

In a **reflection** of a point over a line, the point is flipped so that it is on the opposite side of the line and the same distance from the line.

When a point is reflected across the x-axis, the x-coordinate stays the same and the y-coordinate is changed to its opposite.

When a point is reflected across the y-axis, the y-coordinate stays the same and the x-coordinate is changed to its opposite.

opposite side.

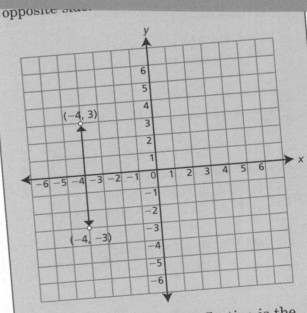

The x-coordinate of the reflection is the same as the x-coordinate of the original point. The y-coordinate of the reflection is the opposite of the y-coordinate of the original point.

14 Warren and Miguel are putting a fence around a garden. They know that the length is 3 more than twice the width. State the length as an expression in terms of the width. Then find the total length of fence they will need if the width is 20 feet. Use $P = 2l + 2w$ to find the total length of fence.

Step 1

So we have $l = \boxed{}\, w + \boxed{}$.

The equation is _____ .

Step 2

$l = 2\, \boxed{} + 3$ or $l =$ _____

The length of the garden is _____ feet.

Step 3

$P = 2\, \underset{\text{length}}{\boxed{}} + 2\, \underset{\text{width}}{\boxed{}}$

Warren and Miguel need _____ feet of fencing to go around the garden.

Step-By-Step

*To solve **example 14**, I must write an expression to represent l using the width. Then I can use the actual width to find the length of the garden and the total fencing needed to go around the garden.*

1 First, I'll write the length in terms of the width. I know from the problem that the length is 3 more than twice the width. I know that 3 more means to add, and twice means to multiply by 2. I will write the equation.

2 Since the width is 20 feet, I know $w = 20$. For the expression $2w + 3$, I can find the length by substituting the value of w and performing the calculations.

3 Finally, I can use the formula for perimeter, or $P = 2l + 2w$, to find the total length of fencing needed.

GO ON

20 **Part A:** Joe is painting a wall in his bedroom. He knows that the height is 8 feet, but the length is twice the height plus 1 foot. Write an expression that represents the length of the wall and find the length. Then determine the area of the wall. Show all your work.

Answer: _____

_____

Part B: Joe reads that 1 quart of paint will cover 100 square feet of wall space and costs $15.99. A gallon of the same paint costs $29.99. How much paint will Joe need? What is his best buy? Explain.

Answer: _____

Explanation: _____

_____

_____

_____

21 Paige is trying to determine the area of her bedroom to see if she can fit her bed, dresser, and couch in there comfortably. She will need 40 square feet of space left after she fits in all the funiture. One wall is 2 feet longer than the other. If the shorter wall is 9 feet, what is the area of the room? Her bed and couch are both 24 square feet and her dresser is 8 square feet. Will she have enough room? Use the formula $A = bh$ for the area. Show all your work. Explain your answer.

Answer: _____

Explanation: _____

_____

_____

_____

_____

Go for it!

Test Practice 4: Expressions

Estimated time: 20 minutes

Directions: Read and answer each question.

1 Which is equivalent to 5^3?

Ⓐ $3 \times 3 \times 3$

Ⓑ $3 \times 3 \times 3 \times 3 \times 3$

Ⓒ 5×3

Ⓓ $5 \times 5 \times 5$

2 Lupe's dog is 10 inches taller than Sarah's dog. The variable s stands for the height of Sarah's dog. Which expression stands for the height of Lupe's dog?

Ⓐ $10s$ Ⓒ $s + 10$

Ⓑ $10 - s$ Ⓓ $s - 10$

3 Kiko baked a batch of cookies. She ate 3 cookies and then gave half of the remaining cookies to her friends. If c represents the number of cookies that Kiko baked, which expression shows the number of cookies she gave to her friends?

Ⓐ $(c - 3) \div 2$

Ⓑ $(c - 2) \div 3$

Ⓒ $c \div 2 - 3$

Ⓓ $c - 3 \div 2$

4 What is the constant in the expression $\frac{t}{5} - 3s + 9$?

Answer: _____

5 What is the value of this expression when $t = 3$ and $r = 15$?

$$90 \div (10 \times t) + r$$

Ⓐ 2 Ⓒ 30

Ⓑ 18 Ⓓ 42

6 Which is not equivalent to $2 \times 2 \times 2 \times 4 \times 4$?

Ⓐ 128

Ⓑ 2^7

Ⓒ $2^3 \times 4^2$

Ⓓ $2^4 \times 3^2$

7 Which expression represents the phrase *5 times a number divided by 8*?

Ⓐ $8n \div 5$ Ⓒ $\frac{5n}{8}$

Ⓑ $\frac{5}{8} + n$ Ⓓ $5n \times 8$

8 Carl used 24 blocks to build a tower. Each block is a cube with a side length of 2 inches. Use the formula $V = s^3$ to find the volume of a cube. What is the volume of the tower?

Answer: _____

9 Which expression is equivalent to $18s - 27t$?

Ⓐ $9 \times 2(s - t)$

Ⓑ $9(2s - 3t)$

Ⓒ $6(3s - 4t)$

Ⓓ $6 \times 3(s - t)$

10 What is the exponential form of $4 \times 4 \times 4$?

Ⓐ 4×3 Ⓒ 3^4

Ⓑ 4^3 Ⓓ 64

11 What is the coefficient of y^2 in the expression $(3y^2 + 9)5$?

Answer: _____

GO ON

12 Evaluate this expression for $x = 10$, $y = 4$, and $z = 2$.

$$(8y - 2)x \div (z + y)$$

Ⓐ 1   Ⓒ 50

Ⓑ 10   Ⓓ 154

13 What is the value of $4m + 2$ when $m = 8$?

Ⓐ 14   Ⓒ 40

Ⓑ 34   Ⓓ 50

14 A boxing ring is a square with 18-foot sides. Use the formula $A = s^2$. What is the area of the boxing ring?

Answer: _____

15 What is the value of 3^4?

Answer: _____

16 Simplify this expression.

$$3y + 6y + 8y$$

Answer: _____

17 Brittney is 4 years older than Dakota. The variable b stands for Brittney's age. Which expression stands for Dakota's age?

Ⓐ $4b$ Ⓒ $b + 4$

Ⓑ $4 - b$ Ⓓ $b - 4$

18 Which expression is equivalent to $8y + 5x - 3y + 7 - 2x$?

Ⓐ $5y + 3x + 7$

Ⓑ $11y - 3x + 7$

Ⓒ $5y - 5x - 7$

Ⓓ $11y + 7x - 7$

19 Simplify this expression for $x = 2$ and $y = 4$.

$$(y + 10x) \div 8 + y^2 - 5$$

Answer: _____

20 Find the surface area of a box that is 15 inches high, 20 inches wide, and 30 inches long. Use the formula $SA = 2 \times (lw + hw + lh)$. Explain how you do it.

Answer: _____

Explanation: _____

_____

_____

_____

_____

_____

_____

Number Correct/Total = _____ /20

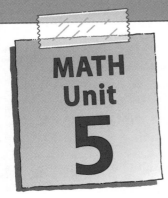

MATH Unit 5

Equations and Inequalities

1 Writing Equations [**6.EE.6, 6.EE.7**]

2 Solving Equations [**6.EE.5, 6.EE.7**]

3 Writing Inequalities [**6.EE.8**]

4 Solutions for Inequalities [**6.EE.5, 6.EE.8**]

5 Two-Variable Equations [**6.EE.6, 6.EE.9**]

Unit 5 Application [**6.EE.5, 6.EE.6, 6.EE.7, 6.EE.8, 6.EE.9**]

Directions: Read and answer each question.

Writing Equations

1 Scott scored a total of 26 points during his last basketball game. He scored 12 points in the first half. Write an equation that can be used to find the number of points he scored in the second half.

Answer: _____

2 Naomi earns $11 an hour. She earned $88 today. Which equation can be used to find the number of hours Naomi worked?

Ⓐ $11 + h = $88

Ⓑ $88 − $11 = h

Ⓒ $h ÷ 11 = $88

Ⓓ $11 × h = $88

Step-By-Step

An equation shows that two expressions have the same value. For **example 1**, write two equivalent expressions with an equal sign between them.

1 The total number of points is 26. Write 26 on one side of the equal sign.

$$\underline{\hspace{1cm}} =$$

2 The total number of points is equal to the number of points scored in the first half plus the number of points scored in the second half. Use the variable p to represent the number of points scored in the second half.

$$26 = \underline{\hspace{1cm}} + p$$

Think It Through

For **example 2**, $11 times the number of hours Naomi worked equals $88, the amount earned.

Use h to represent the number of hours. Then $11 times h equals $88.

In symbols, that is

[   ].

Solving Equations

3 Find the value of t in this equation.

$$t - 12 = 20$$

   Ⓐ $t = 32$ Ⓒ $t = -8$

   Ⓑ $t = 8$ Ⓓ $t = -32$

Remember . . .

You can solve equations using **inverse operations**.

   To undo addition, subtract.

   To undo subtraction, add.

   To undo multiplication, divide.

   To undo division, multiply.

4 Solve for p.

$$4 \times p = 112$$

   Ⓐ $p = 23$ Ⓒ $p = 48$

   Ⓑ $p = 28$ Ⓓ $p = 448$

Another Way

Another way to find the value of p that makes the equation true is to substitute each answer choice into the equation.

Step-By-Step

To find the value of t in **example 3**, undo subtraction by adding. Keep the equation balanced by adding the same number to both sides of the equation.

1 Add 12 to both sides of the equation.

$$t - 12 = 20$$

$$t - 12 + 12 = 20 + 12$$

2 Simplify.

$$t = 20 + 12$$

$$t = \boxed{}$$

Step-By-Step

For **example 4**, you need to get p alone on one side of the equal sign. p is multiplied by 4. To undo multiplication, use the inverse operation, or division.

1 Divide both sides of the equation by 4.

$$4 \times p = 112$$

$$4 \div 4 \times p = 112 \div 4$$

2 Simplify.

$$p = 112 \div 4$$

$$p = \boxed{}$$

1 $t - 15 = 4$

$t = $ _____

2 $15 - q = 4$

$q = $ _____

3 $\frac{a}{5} = 40$

$a = $ _____

4 $d \times 5 = 40$

$d = $ _____

5 How can you solve $10 = 2.5g$?

Ⓐ Multiply both sides by 2.5.
Ⓑ Divide both sides by 2.5.
Ⓒ Multiply both sides by 10.
Ⓓ Divide both sides by 10.

6 What is the solution to $6 + k = 5(1.2)$?

Ⓐ 0   Ⓒ 2
Ⓑ 1   Ⓓ 12

7 Write an equation that has 2 as its solution. Use the variable n.

Answer: _____

8 Choose the equation with the greatest solution.

Ⓐ $y + 5 = 14$
Ⓑ $26 \div c = 2$
Ⓒ $6 \times w = 72$
Ⓓ $27 - p = 17$

9 Which of these equations is NOT true?

Ⓐ $36 \div 3 = 2 \times 6$
Ⓑ $4 \times 6 = 30 - 5$
Ⓒ $9 + 9 = 3 \times 6$
Ⓓ $13 + 7 = 100 \div 5$

10 Which number makes this equation true?

$$3(12 - g) = g + 8$$

Ⓐ 3   Ⓒ 7
Ⓑ 4   Ⓓ 12

GO ON

5 In the United States, a person 18 years or older can vote. Which inequality shows age (*a*) 18 or older?

 Ⓐ $a > 18$

 Ⓑ $a \geq 18$

 Ⓒ $a < 18$

 Ⓓ $a \leq 18$

Inequality Symbols

$>$ means **is greater than.**

$<$ means **is less than.**

$\geq$ means **is greater than or equal to.**

$\leq$ means **is less than or equal to.**

6 Write an inequality for the following statement.

2 times a number plus 1 is less than 9

Answer: _____

Think It Through

For **example 5**, you need to show an age (*a*) greater than or equal to 18 years. Use the *Inequality Symbols* box to choose the symbol for greater than or equal to.

$$a \boxed{} 18$$

Step-By-Step

In **example 6**, let *n* stand for the unknown number.

Replace the phrase *is less than* with $<$ and *a number* with *n*.

2 times a *number* plus 1 *is less than* 9

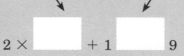

$$2 \times \boxed{} + 1 \boxed{} 9$$

Solutions for Inequalities

7 Which number is a solution to the inequality $n < -2$?

  Ⓐ 2

  Ⓑ 0

  Ⓒ −2

  Ⓓ −4

8 Which number line shows the solution set for the inequality $y \geq 2$?

Ⓐ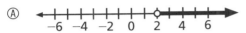

Ⓑ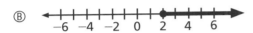

Ⓒ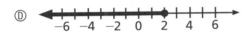

Ⓓ

Graphing Inequalities

Use a closed circle to show that a number is included in the solution.

$$n \geq 3$$

n is greater than or equal to 3

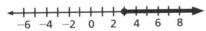

Use an open circle to show that the number is not a part of the solution.

$$n > 3$$

n is greater than 3

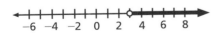

Step-By-Step

For **example 7**, use substitution to find the number that is less than −2.

1 Substitute each number into the inequality $n < -2$.

    Let $n = 2$. Is $2 < -2$ true? _____

    Let $n = 0$. Is $0 < -2$ true? _____

    Let $n = -2$. Is $-2 < -2$ true? _____

    Let $n = -4$. Is $-4 < -2$ true? _____

2 Choose the answer that makes the inequality true.

The inequality $y \geq 2$ in **example 8** has an infinite number of solutions. You can show them by graphing the inequality on a number line.

1 The solution to $y \geq 2$ includes all numbers greater than or equal to 2. Which two answer choices show the graph of numbers greater than 2?

    [ ] and [ ]

2 Look at the circles. A solid circle includes 2 in the solution. Which answer choice shows all numbers greater than or equal to 2?

    [ ]

11 Which number is a solution to the inequality $2n \geq 12$?

    Ⓐ 3   Ⓒ 5

    Ⓑ 4   Ⓓ 6

12 Write an inequality for the statement below. Then use the number line to show the solution set for the inequality.

2 plus a number is less than or equal to 7.

Answer: _____

Two-Variable Equations

9 The DollarWise Baseball Store is having a sale. Study the advertisement below. Which equation could be used to find the cost of any pair of items? Let x equal the price of one item; let c equal the total cost.

The DollarWise Baseball Store   BIG SALE

Buy a pair of any item and get a dollar off!

Hats	$2 each
Balls	$5 each
Bats	$10 each
Gloves	$12 each

    Ⓐ $c = 2x - 1$ Ⓒ $c = x + 1$

    Ⓑ $c = 2x + 1$ Ⓓ $c = x - 1$

Step-By-Step

An algebraic equation shows the equal relationship between two expressions. In **example 9**, the ad says that if you buy 2 of any item, you will get $1 off the regular price.

1 How would you find the cost of buying 2 hats?

$$\text{Total cost} = 2(\$2) - \$1$$

2 Rewrite the equation using variables. Let c stand for the total cost and x stand for the price of the item.

$$c = 2x - 1$$

3 Be sure to check that the equation works for every situation in the problem.

Two-Variable Equations

10 The table shows the number of pounds of dog food left from a 50-pound bag at the end of each day.

Day (d)	Number of Pounds (p)
0	50
1	48
2	46
3	44
4	42

Write an equation that can be used to find the number of pounds of dog food (p) remaining at the end of d days.

Answer: _____

Step-By-Step

For **example 10**, the number of pounds of dog food left depends on the number of days that have passed. The number of days is the independent variable. The number of pounds is the dependent variable.

1 The table shows that p decreases by 2 each day. The decrease for any number of days can be found by multiplying the number of days (d) by 2. Write 2 times the number of days in symbols.

$$2\ \boxed{}$$

2 The number of pounds (p) of dog food left can be found by subtracting 2d from 50 pounds.

$$p = \boxed{} - 2d$$

GO ON

Two-Variable Equations

11   Nick made this graph to describe his hike so far.

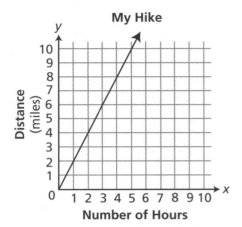

My Hike

If Nick continues at the same rate, how far will he walk in 8 hours?

Ⓐ 4 miles

Ⓑ 10 miles

Ⓒ 12 miles

Ⓓ 16 miles

Step-By-Step

To solve **example 11**, find the relationship between the number of hours and the distance hiked.

1 Make a table and fill in the distance hiked for each number of hours.

Hours	Distance (miles)
1	2
2	4
3	6
4	8
5	10

2 Compare the hours to the distances to figure out the pattern.

$$1 \times 2 = 2 \quad 4 \times 2 = 8$$
$$2 \times 2 = 4 \quad 5 \times 2 = 10$$
$$3 \times 2 = 6$$

The distance is two times the number of hours.

$$d = 2h$$

3 Multiply to find how many miles Nick will hike in 8 hours.

$$d = 2h$$

$$d = 2 \times 8 = \boxed{}$$

Try It

13   What is the value of $xy - y$?

$$x = 3 \quad y = 5$$

Answer: _____

14   Evaluate the following expression for $h = 4$ and $k = 2$.

$$h^2 - 5k$$

Answer: _____

15   Which sentence describes the rule for the table?

x	y
0	2
1	5
2	8
3	11

Ⓐ $y = x + 2$ Ⓒ $y = x + 6$

Ⓑ $y = x \times 5$ Ⓓ $y = 3x + 2$

12 **Part A:** Alli plants trees for her neighbors. She charges $9.75 per tree. Write an equation to represent her earnings from planting trees.

Step 1

$$\underline{\hspace{2cm}} = \underline{\hspace{2cm}} \times \underline{\hspace{2cm}}$$
earnings   charge for   number of trees
         planting one tree

Part B: She is saving up for a spring break trip and needs to make at least $200 in order to go. Rewrite the equation as an inequality and solve to determine how many trees she will need to plant to go on the trip.

Step 2

$9.75N \geq \underline{\hspace{3cm}}$
        amount she must
            earn

Step 3

Solve: $9.75N \geq $200

Alli must plant at least _____ trees to go on her spring break trip.

Step-By-Step

*To solve **example 12**, first I will write an equation to show Alli's earnings. Then I will write the inequality that matches how many trees she must plant in order for her to attend her trip.*

1 I know that she plants trees for $9.75. If *e* equals Alli's earnings and *N* equals the number of trees she plants, I can write the equation.

2 Now, I know that Alli needs to make at least $200 to go on the trip. When I use the phrase "at least," I know I will be writing an inequality. Alli's earnings need to be "equal to or greater than" $200. I can use the expression for earnings from Part A, the amount she must earn, and the inequality ($\geq$) to write the equation.

3 Since division is the inverse of multiplication, I can solve by dividing by 9.75.

GO ON

16 Tucker the dog weighs 8 lbs and is gaining 2 lbs a week. Write an equation to determine his weight after a certain number of weeks. If his breed rarely weighs more than 60 lbs, determine in how many weeks he will reach 60 lbs if he stays with this trend. Show all of your work.

Answer: _____

17 Keisha is trying to read 3 books a week to win the book-reading contest. She has already read 15 books and believes she needs to read 40 books to win. Write an equation and solve to determine how many weeks Keisha will need to maintain her rate of reading.

Answer: _____

18 Rashida is going to be buying presents for her friends this holiday season. She wants to spend $10 on each of her friends and $5 on herself. She knows she cannot spend more than $50 total. Write and solve an inequality to determine how many friends she can buy for.

Answer: _____

19 Amir is saving money for a new mountain bike that costs $800. He has already saved $100. He earns $50 per week working as a counselor with elementary kids in the after-school program. How many weeks will it take Amir to save enough to buy the bike? Make a table showing the week number (w) and Amir's total savings (s).

Answer: _____

Go for it!

Test Practice 5: Equations and Inequalities

Estimated time: 25 minutes

Directions: Read and answer each question.

1 Choose the value for k that makes this equation true.

$$80 = 5k$$

- Ⓐ $k = 16$
- Ⓒ $k = 85$
- Ⓑ $k = 75$
- Ⓓ $k = 400$

2 Which number line shows the solution set for the inequality $h \leq 1$?

Ⓐ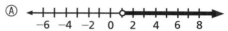

Ⓑ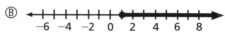

Ⓒ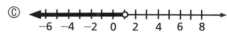

Ⓓ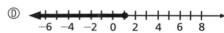

3 Kiko swims every day at the gym. She can swim 2 miles in an hour. Let y equal the number of miles and x equal the total time in hours. Which equation shows how many miles Kiko can swim in x hours?

- Ⓐ $y = x + 1$
- Ⓒ $y = 2x$
- Ⓑ $y = 2x + 1$
- Ⓓ $y = x - 2$

4 Graph the inequality $x < 4$ on this number line.

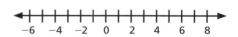

5 Choose the value for r that makes this equation true.

$$r - 6.7 = 9$$

- Ⓐ $r = 15.7$
- Ⓒ $r = 3.7$
- Ⓑ $r = 2.3$
- Ⓓ $r = 60.3$

6 Write an inequality for the following statement.

6 times a number plus 4 is greater than 50

Answer: _____

7 At a factory, 450 bottles of ketchup are produced each hour. Which equation can be used to show the relationship between time in hours (h) and the number of bottles (b) of ketchup produced?

- Ⓐ $450 \div h = b$
- Ⓑ $450h = b$
- Ⓒ $450 + b = h$
- Ⓓ $450b = h$

8 Emily started a savings account with $40. She drew this graph of her savings over 7 months.

Which equation can be used to find the amount (a) of Emily's savings for any month (m)?

- Ⓐ $a = 20m$
- Ⓒ $a = 40m$
- Ⓑ $a = 20m + 40$
- Ⓓ $a = 40m + 20$

GO ON

9 To pass an exam, you need to get more than 60 points. Write the inequality that shows a score (*s*) greater than 60 points.

Answer: _____

10 Joshua had $860. He used $500 to pay his rent. Which equation can be used to find *a*, the amount he has left?

Ⓐ $a + \$500 = \$860$

Ⓑ $a + \$860 = \$500$

Ⓒ $\$860 + \$500 = a$

Ⓓ $\$500 - a = \$860$

11 Which value of *x* makes the inequality $x < -3$ true?

Ⓐ -4

Ⓑ -2

Ⓒ 0

Ⓓ 2

12 Write the equation that represents *6 less than 2 times a number equals 4.*

Answer: _____

13 At least 16 students must sign up for a geology class or the class will be cancelled. Let *s* be the number of students. Write an inequality to represent this situation.

Answer: _____

14 How can you solve $23 = n - 9$?

Ⓐ Add 9 to both sides.

Ⓑ Subtract 9 from both sides.

Ⓒ Add 23 to both sides.

Ⓓ Subtract 23 from both sides.

15 How many solutions does the inequality shown on this number line have?

Ⓐ an infinite number

Ⓑ 15

Ⓒ 9

Ⓓ 1

16 The maximum weight a picture hook can hold is 10 pounds. Which inequality represents this situation?

Ⓐ $w \leq 10$

Ⓑ $w < 10$

Ⓒ $w \geq 10$

Ⓓ $w > 10$

17 Solve for *p*.

$$\tfrac{1}{6} + p = 2\tfrac{1}{2}$$

Ⓐ $2\tfrac{1}{6}$ Ⓒ $2\tfrac{2}{3}$

Ⓑ $2\tfrac{1}{3}$ Ⓓ $2\tfrac{5}{6}$

18 Use this table. Write an equation that can be used to find the number of feet, *f*, of wood needed for any number of bookcases, *b*.

Number of Bookcases	Number of Feet of Wood
1	24
2	48
3	72
4	96
5	120

Answer: _____

19 Solve for *b*. Show your work.

$$24 \div b = 6$$

Answer: _____

20 Renting a bicycle at Best Bikes costs $5 an hour plus $3 for a helmet. Complete this table to show the cost of renting a bicycle. Then fill in the graph to show the data and write an equation showing the relationship between cost (*c*) and number of hours (*h*).

Answer: _____

Number of Hours (*h*)	Cost (*c*)

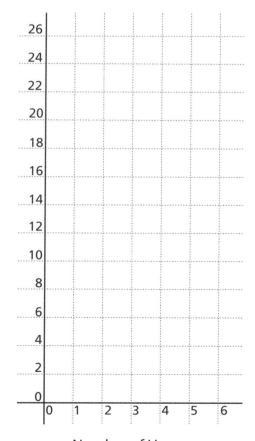

Cost

Number of Hours

Number Correct/Total = _____/20

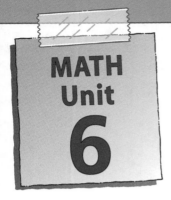

Measurement and Geometry

1 Area of Triangles **[6.G.1]**

2 Area of Quadrilaterals **[6.G.1]**

3 Area of Polygons **[6.G.1]**

4 Volume of Rectangular Prisms **[6.G.2]**

5 Polygons in the Coordinate Plane **[6.G.3]**

6 Surface Area **[6.G.4]**

Unit 6 Application **[6.G.1, 6.G.4]**

Directions: Read and answer each question.

Area of Triangles

1 What is the area of the white part of this flag?

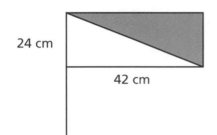

24 cm

42 cm

Ⓐ 132 cm²

Ⓑ 504 cm²

Ⓒ 576 cm²

Ⓓ 1,008 cm²

Step-By-Step

The flag in **example 1** is a rectangle. The white part of the flag is $\frac{1}{2}$ of the rectangle.

1 The base of the rectangle is 42 cm. The height is 24 cm. Use the formula $A = bh$ to find the area of the rectangle.

$$A = 42 \times \boxed{}$$

2 Multiply the area of the rectangle by $\frac{1}{2}$ to find the area of the white part of the flag.

$$A = \tfrac{1}{2} \times 1{,}008 = \boxed{} \text{ cm}^2$$

Area of Triangles

2 What is the area of the triangle shown below?

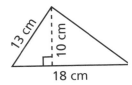

13 cm   10 cm
18 cm

Ⓐ 42 cm²
Ⓑ 71.5 cm²
Ⓒ 90 cm²
Ⓓ 117 cm²

Step-By-Step

The formula $A = \frac{1}{2}bh$ can be used to find the area of any triangle. Use the formula to find the area for **example 2**.

1 The height of a triangle is perpendicular to the base and passes through the opposite vertex. Identify the base and height of the triangle.

$$b = \boxed{} \qquad h = \boxed{}$$

2 Substitute the measurements into the formula.

$$A = \frac{1}{2}bh$$

$$A = \frac{1}{2}(18 \times \boxed{})$$

3 Multiply.

$$A = \frac{1}{2}(18 \times 10)$$

$$A = \frac{1}{2}(\boxed{})$$

$$A = \boxed{}$$

Try It

1 Solve for the area of the shaded part of the rectangle below. Show your work.

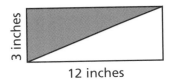

3 inches
12 inches

Answer: _____

Answer the following questions using the triangle shown.

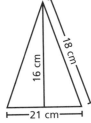

16 cm   18 cm
├─ 21 cm ─┤

2 What is the base?

Answer: _____

3 What is the height?

Answer: _____

4 What is the area?

Answer: _____

3 The design for a garden in the shape of a parallelogram is shown below. There is a 10-foot-long path across the garden.

20 ft

10 ft

12 ft

What is the area of the garden?

Ⓐ 64 ft^2 Ⓒ 200 ft^2

Ⓑ 120 ft^2 Ⓓ 240 ft^2

Think It Through

Think of cutting apart the parallelogram in **example 3** and making it into a rectangle.

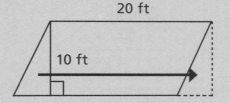

20 ft

10 ft

The area formulas for rectangles and parallelograms are the same—area equals base times height.

Use the formula $A = bh$ to find the area of the garden.

$$A = 20 \times 10 = \boxed{} \text{ ft}^2$$

Areas of Parallelograms and Triangles

The diagonal separates the parallelogram below into two equal triangles. The area of one of the triangles is $\frac{1}{2}$ the area of the parallelogram.

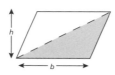

Area of parallelogram = bh

Area of triangle = $\frac{1}{2}bh$

Triangle and Parallelogram Height

The height of a triangle or parallelogram is the perpendicular distance from the base to the opposite vertex. Height is sometimes called *altitude* (*a*).

 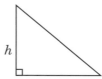 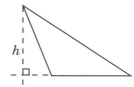 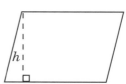

4 What is the area of the trapezoid shown below?

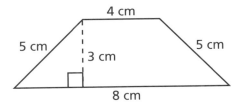

Ⓐ 18 cm^2

Ⓑ 22 cm^2

Ⓒ 25 cm^2

Ⓓ 40 cm^2

Area Formulas

Parallelogram

$$A = \text{base} \times \text{height}$$

Trapezoid

$$A = \tfrac{1}{2}(\text{sum of bases}) \times \text{height}$$

Step-By-Step

Use the following formula to find the area of a trapezoid as in **example 4**.

$$A = \tfrac{1}{2}(b_1 + b_2) \times h$$

1 The 3 cm length is the height of the trapezoid because it is the length of the perpendicular distance between the parallel sides.

$$\text{height} = 3 \text{ cm}$$

2 The bases are the parallel sides.

$$\text{base}_1 = 4 \text{ cm} \qquad \text{base}_2 = 8 \text{ cm}$$

3 Multiply half the sum of the bases times the height.

$$A = \tfrac{1}{2}(\text{sum of the bases}) \times \text{height}$$

$$A = 6 \text{ cm} \times 3 \text{ cm} = \boxed{} \text{ cm}^2$$

Another Way

Divide the trapezoid into triangles.

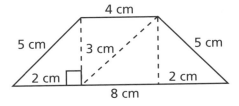

Find the area of the triangles.

5 Mr. Evans is planning to put linoleum on his kitchen floor. The dimensions of his kitchen are shown below.

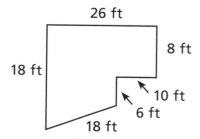

26 ft
8 ft
18 ft
10 ft
6 ft
18 ft

How many square feet of linoleum does he need to cover the entire floor?
(The formula for the area of a trapezoid is $A = \frac{1}{2}(b_1 + b_2) \times h$.)

Ⓐ 128 ft^2 Ⓒ 336 ft^2

Ⓑ 208 ft^2 Ⓓ 468 ft^2

Finding the Area of Polygons

Many polygons can be divided into familiar shapes, such as squares, rectangles, and triangles.

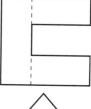

3 rectangles

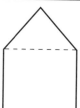

1 square

1 triangle

Step-By-Step

Follow these steps to solve **example 5**.

1 Divide the figure into 2 quadrilaterals. Notice how the dotted line forms a rectangle and a trapezoid.

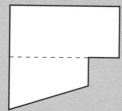

2 Find the side lengths of the rectangle. Subtract as necessary to find the side lengths of the trapezoid.

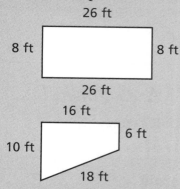

26 ft
8 ft   8 ft
26 ft

16 ft
10 ft   6 ft
18 ft

3 Find the area of the rectangle.

$$A = l \times w$$
$$A = 26 \times 8$$
$$A = \boxed{} \text{ ft}^2$$

4 Find the area of the trapezoid. Remember that the bases are the parallel sides.

$$A = \frac{1}{2}(b_1 + b_2) \times h$$
$$A = \frac{1}{2}(10 + 6) \times 16$$
$$A = \boxed{} \text{ ft}^2$$

5 Add to find the total area of the shape.

$$208 \text{ ft}^2 + 128 \text{ ft}^2 = \boxed{} \text{ ft}^2$$

Volume of Rectangular Prisms

6 This rectangular prism is built with cubes that are $\frac{1}{5}$ inch on a side.

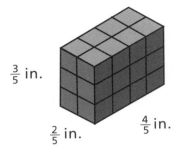

$\frac{3}{5}$ in.

$\frac{2}{5}$ in.

$\frac{4}{5}$ in.

What is the volume of the rectangular prism?

Answer: _____

Another Way

You can find the volume of the rectangular prism by multiplying its length times its width times its height.

$$V = \frac{4}{5} \times \frac{2}{5} \times \frac{3}{5} = \frac{24}{125}$$

Step-By-Step

Volume is the amount of space a solid figure occupies. It is measured in cubic units. For **example 6**, the volume of the rectangular prism is measured in cubic inches.

1 Each of the cubes that makes up the rectangular prism is $\frac{1}{5}$ inch on a side.

$\frac{1}{5}$ in.

$\frac{1}{5}$ in. $\frac{1}{5}$ in.

Find the volume of 1 cube. Use the formula $V = s^3$ where s is the side length.

$$V = s^3 = \frac{1}{5} \times \frac{1}{5} \times \frac{1}{5} = \frac{\boxed{}}{125}$$

2 Count the number of cubes in one layer of the rectangular prism. Then multiply by the volume of a cube to find the volume of one layer.

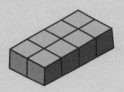

$$8 \times \frac{1}{125} = \frac{\boxed{}}{125} \text{ in.}^3$$

3 Count the number of layers. Multiply the number of layers by the volume of one layer.

$$3 \times \frac{8}{125} = \frac{\boxed{}}{125} \text{ in.}^3$$

Volume of Rectangular Prisms

7 A mini-flashlight is in the shape of a rectangular prism. It is $\frac{3}{8}$ in. wide, $1\frac{1}{4}$ in. tall, and $\frac{5}{8}$ in. long. What is its volume?

Answer: _____

Volume of a Rectangular Prism

$V = Bh$

$V = (\text{area of the base}) \times \text{height}$

$V = (l \times w) \times h$

Step-By-Step

For **example 7**, write each number as a fraction. Then use the formula $V = l \times w \times h$ to find the volume.

1 Write $1\frac{1}{4}$ as an improper fraction.

$$1\frac{1}{4} = \frac{5}{\boxed{}}$$

2 Substitute the dimensions into the formula. Then multiply.

$$V = l \times w \times h$$

$$V = \frac{5}{8} \times \frac{3}{8} \times \frac{5}{4}$$

$$V = \frac{\boxed{}}{256} \text{ in.}^3$$

Try It

5 Find the area of a parallelogram with a base of 12 cm and height of 5 cm.

Answer: _____

6 Find the area of the trapezoid shown.

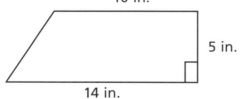

Answer: _____

7 Find the area of the polygon shown.

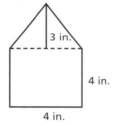

Show your work in the space below.

Answer: _____

8 Fred is finding the volume of a shoe box with dimensions of 5 in., 6 in., and 14 in. He uses one 5-by-6 face as the base. What should he use for the height?

Answer: _____

9

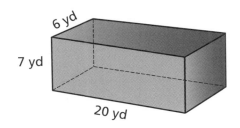

Area of base: _____

Volume: _____

10 Fill in the missing length on the figure below. Then find the area of the figure. Write your answer on the line provided.

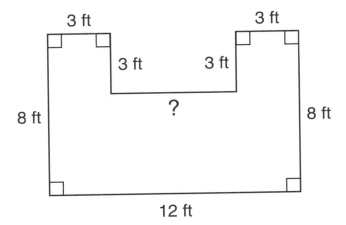

Answer: _____

GO ON

Open-Ended Practice

Some tests include questions in which you must explain how you solved a problem. You may also be asked to show your work, draw graphs, or make diagrams. The example below will give you practice responding to such questions.

Polygons in the Coordinate Plane

8   On the grid below, plot and label point *A* at (3, 3) and point *B* at (3, 7). Then follow the directions for Part A and answer Part B.

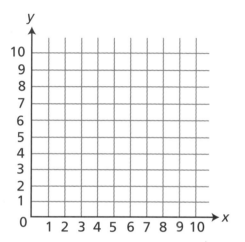

Part A

Plot point *C* so that, when connected, points *A*, *B*, and *C* form an isosceles right triangle called △*ABC*.

Part B

What is the ordered pair for point *C*?

Answer: _____

Step-By-Step

Example 8 has two parts. Be sure to answer all parts of open-ended items and to show and label your work clearly. Follow the steps for one way to answer this problem.

1   First plot and label points *A* and *B*. Remember, the first number of a coordinate pair tells you the number of units to the right to move; the second number tells you the number of units to move up.

2   You are to form an isosceles triangle—a triangle with two equal sides. Connect points *A* and *B*. Then count the number of units in $\overline{AB}$. Draw $\overline{BC}$ so that it is the same length as $\overline{AB}$ and forms a right angle.

3   Connect $\overline{BC}$ and $\overline{CA}$ to form the triangle.

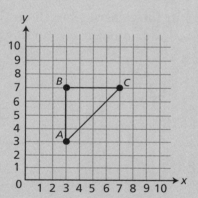

4   To answer Part B, find the ordered pair for point *C*.

9 Rosa drew this coordinate grid to show her backyard. The side of each square is 1 meter.

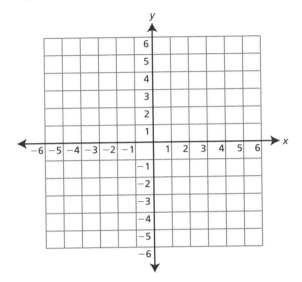

Plot the points $(-5, 4)$, $(-5, -2)$, $(3, -2)$, and $(3, 4)$ and connect them to show Rosa's garden. What is the perimeter of the garden?

Answer: _____

Remember . . .

When two points have the same *x*-coordinate, you can find the distance between them by adding the absolute values of the *y*-coordinates.

When two points have the same *y*-coordinate, you can find the distance between them by adding the absolute values of the *x*-coordinates.

Step-By-Step

For **example 9**, plot the points then find the distances between them.

1 Plot the points $(-5, 4)$, $(-5, -2)$, $(3, -2)$, and $(3, 4)$ and connect them in order.

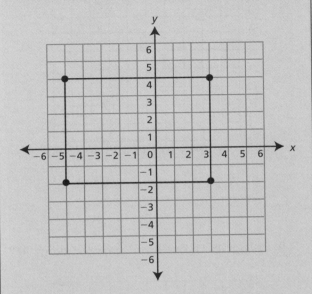

2 Find the length and width of the rectangle.

Length = _____ meters

Width = _____ meters

3 Find the perimeter of the rectangular garden. Substitute the length and width into the perimeter formula.

$P = 2l + 2w$

$P = 2(8) + 2(6)$

$P =$ _____ meters

GO ON ▷

11 Which point is located at (36, 10)?

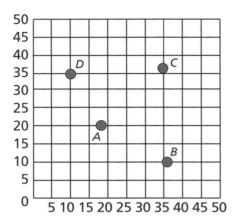

ⓐ *A*   ⓒ *C*

ⓑ *B*   ⓓ *D*

12 What is the ordered pair for point *M*?

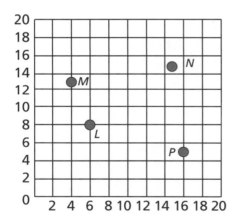

ⓐ (5, 13)   ⓒ (4, 13)

ⓑ (6, 8)   ⓓ (15, 15)

13 The ordered pairs for three vertices of a square have been plotted on this coordinate grid.

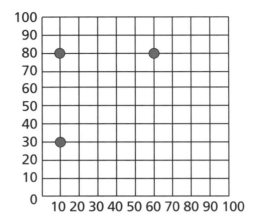

Plot the fourth point and name the ordered pair.

Answer: _____

14 Use the coordinates below to plot points on the grid. Beginning with point *A*, connect the points and name the geometric figure you have drawn.

Point	Coordinates
A	(6, 4)
B	(4, 10)
C	(10, 12)
D	(16, 10)
E	(14, 4)

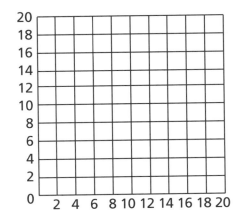

Answer: _____

Surface Area

10 This net can be folded to make a rectangular prism. The prism is 5 units tall, 3 units wide, and 2 units deep.

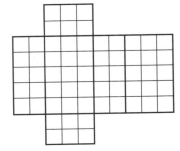 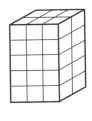

What is the surface area of the prism?

Ⓐ 62 units^2

Ⓑ 52 units^2

Ⓒ 48 units^2

Ⓓ 30 units^2

Step-By-Step

Surface area is the sum of the areas of all surfaces of a solid figure. It is described with square units such as square centimeters (cm^2) or square inches (in.^{2}). Follow these steps to find the surface area for **example 10**.

1 Find the area of each face.

$$\text{top} = (3 \times 2) = 6 \text{ units}^2$$

$$\text{bottom} = (3 \times 2) = 6 \text{ units}^2$$

$$\text{front} = (3 \times 5) = 15 \text{ units}^2$$

$$\text{back} = (3 \times 5) = 15 \text{ units}^2$$

$$\text{right side} = (2 \times 5) = 10 \text{ units}^2$$

$$\text{back side} = (2 \times 5) = 10 \text{ units}^2$$

2 Add the areas of all the faces. To simplify, use multiplication as shown below.

$$2(6) + 2(15) + 2(10) = \boxed{}$$

GO ON →

Surface Area

11 Bella's Bakery is planning to use this box to package new crackers.

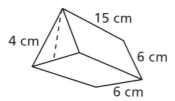

What is the area of the cardboard needed to make the box?

Answer: _____ cm²

Try It

15 This net can be folded up to make a triangular prism. What is the volume of the prism?

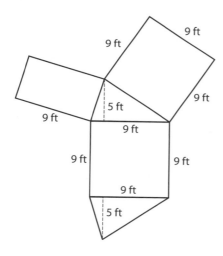

Answer: _____

Step-By-Step

To help you find the surface area of the box in **example 11**, draw a net.

1 Draw a net for the box.

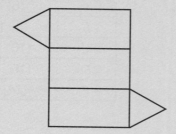

2 The rectangles are each 6 cm wide and 15 cm long. Find the area of a rectangle and then multiply by 3.

A (rectangle) $= l \times w$

$A = 6 \times 15 = $ ☐ cm²

A (3 rectangles) $= 3 \times 90 = $ ☐ cm²

3 Each triangle has a base of 6 cm and height 4 cm. Find the area of each triangle and then multiply by 2.

A (triangle) $= \frac{1}{2} bh$

$A = \frac{1}{2} \times 6 \times 4 = $ ☐ cm²

A (2 triangles) $= 2 \times 12 = $ ☐ cm²

4 Add the areas of the 3 rectangles and the 2 triangles to find the surface area of the box.

$SA = 270 + 24 = $ ☐ cm²

12 Fancy Furniture makes dollhouses for its younger clients. Below is a print of a basic home that they make. Determine the surface area of the house. Assume that the building has 4 full sides and the roof is included, but there is no need to include the area of the base.

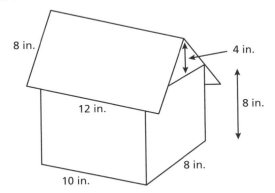

Step 1

Area of half of the roof: $A = l \times w$

Total Area = _____ × _____ × 2

The area of the roof is _____.

Step 2

Area of the large sides: $A = l \times w$

Area of both sides = _____ × _____ × 2

The area of the large sides is _____.

Step 3

Area of the front and back: **triangle** $A = \frac{1}{2} bh$ and **square** $A = l \times w$

$A \triangle = \frac{1}{2}$ _____ × _____ = _____

$A \square =$ _____ × _____ = _____

     triangle   square   Area of front

_____ + _____ = _____ × 2

The area of the front and back is _____.

Step 4

The area of the dollhouse is _____.

Step-By-Step

In order to determine the surface area of the dollhouse, I will need to consider each section separately.

1 First, I'll find the area of the roof. The roof is formed by 2 rectangles. I'll use the formula for finding the area of a rectangle. Since there are 2 sides to the roof, I'll multiply the area by 2.

2 Second, I'll find the area of the large side and multiply by 2 since there are 2 sides.

3 Next, I need to find the area of the front and back, or the 2 sides that have a triangular top, called *gables*. I'll use the triangle formula for that part, which measures 4 inches by 8 inches. Then I'll find the area of the square that is 8 inches by 8 inches. To find the total area, I'll add the two parts. Then since there are a front and a back this size, I need to multiply by 2.

4 Finally I will add all of the areas together.

GO ON

16 Amina wants to send a box to her best friend and needs to wrap it with paper to ship. The box has 2 sides that are 13 inches by 12 inches, 2 sides that are 6 inches by 13 inches, and 2 sides that are 6 inches by 12 inches. How many square inches of paper will she need? How many square feet is that?

Answer: _____

17 Juan is going to be making a square cake for his friend. He is adding a pyramid to the top to make it look like a castle. The dimensions of the base of the cake are 8 × 8 × 3 inches. Each triangle of the pyramid has a base of 4 inches and a height of 3 inches. Find the surface area of the cake so that he knows how much frosting to make to cover the whole cake. He will not cover the bottom of the pyramid.

Answer: _____

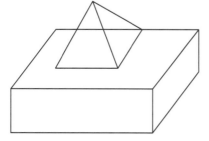

18 Brooklyn paints for people. Her current project is the door below. She must paint all the grey parts blue and all of the white parts green. Find the surface area of each color, so that she knows how much paint to purchase.

Answer: _____

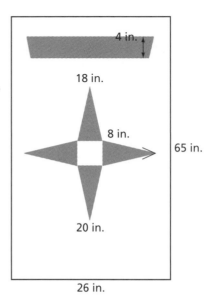

Go for it!

Test Practice 6: Measurement and Geometry

Estimated time: 30 minutes

Directions: Read and answer each question.

1 This rectangular prism is constructed of $\frac{1}{4}$-inch cubes.

What is its volume?

Answer: _____

2 Sea Seasonings is making a box to hold its new Flavors of the Sea seasonings. The box is shown below.

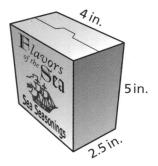

How many square inches of cardboard are needed to make 1 box?

Answer: _____

3 What is the area of this parallelogram?

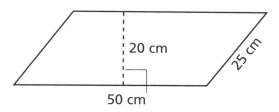

Ⓐ 50 cm^2

Ⓑ 500 cm^2

Ⓒ 1,000 cm^2

Ⓓ 1,250 cm^2

4 Julie made the sign below for her science fair project.

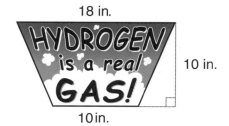

What is the area of the trapezoid?

Ⓐ 140 in.^{2}

Ⓑ 180 in.^{2}

Ⓒ 280 in.^{2}

Ⓓ 1,800 in.^{2}

GO ON ⇨

5 Which is the net for this figure?

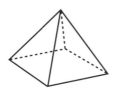

Ⓐ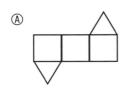

Ⓑ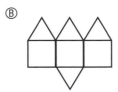

Ⓒ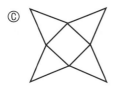

Ⓓ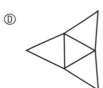

6 Each cube used to make this rectangular prism is $\frac{1}{3}$ of a foot on a side. Which equation can be solved to find the volume of the prism?

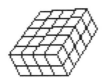

Ⓐ $V = (5 \times 4 \times 2) \frac{1}{27}$

Ⓑ $V = (5 \times 4 \times 2) \, 27$

Ⓒ $V = (5 \times 4 \times 2) \frac{1}{9}$

Ⓓ $V = (5 \times 4 \times 2) \, 9$

7 This is a drawing of Dogsville Park. The path is 80 feet long. The section of Elm Street that borders the park is 60 feet.

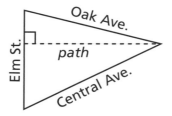

What is the area of Dogsville Park?

Answer: _____

8 This is a map of Cindy's neighborhood. Each square is 1 block.

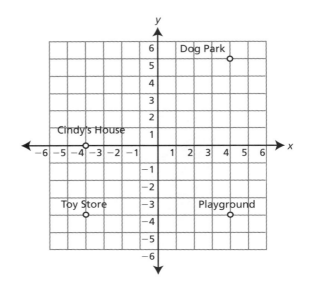

How much farther is it from the dog park to the playground than it is from the playground to the toy store?

Answer: _____

106

9 Alex made this drawing of the deck he wants to build.

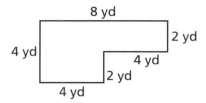

What is the area of the deck?

Answer: _____

10 How many square inches of fabric does George need for a triangular flag with a base of 20 inches and a height of 40 inches?

Ⓐ 100 in.^{2} Ⓒ 400 in.^{2}

Ⓑ 120 in.^{2} Ⓓ 800 in.^{2}

11 What is the area of this banner?

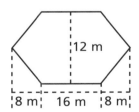

Ⓐ 384 m^2

Ⓑ 288 m^2

Ⓒ 192 m^2

Ⓓ 96 m^2

12 Draw a net for this box. Then find the surface area of the box. Explain how you do it.

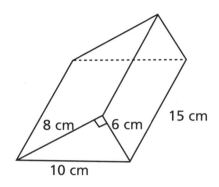

Answer: _____

Explanation: _____

_____

_____

_____

_____

GO ON

13 The ordered pairs for three vertices of a square have been plotted on this coordinate grid.

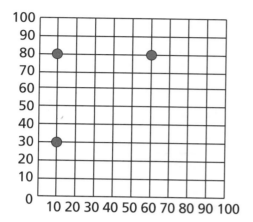

Name the ordered pair for the fourth point.

Answer: _____

14 Alex made this design as part of her art project.

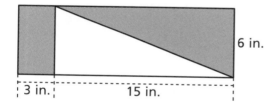

What is the area of the shaded part of the design?

Ⓐ 45 in.²   Ⓒ 90 in.²

Ⓑ 63 in.²   Ⓓ 108 in.²

15 The box for Emma's earrings is $2\frac{1}{2}$ in. long, $1\frac{3}{4}$ in. wide, and $\frac{3}{4}$ in. tall. What is the volume of the box?

Answer: _____

16 Graph these points on the coordinate grid and connect them in order.
(−5, 4) (−5, −5) (2, −5) (2, −2) (6, −2) (6, 4) (−5, 4)

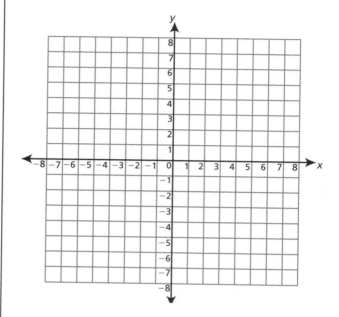

What is the perimeter of the polygon?

Perimeter: _____

What is the area of the polygon?

Area: _____

STOP

Number Correct/Total = _____ /16

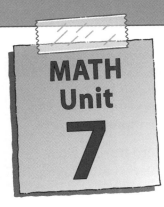

MATH Unit 7

Statistics

1 Statistical Questions [**6.SP.1**]

2 Measures of Center [**6.SP.2, 6.SP.3, 6.SP.5c**]

3 Measures of Variation [**6.SP.2, 6.SP.3, 6.SP.5c**]

4 Displaying and Summarizing Data [**6.SP.4, 6.SP.5a, 6.SP.5b, 6.SP.5d**]

Unit 7 Application [**6.SP.2, 6.SP.3, 6.SP.4, 6.SP.5b, 6.SP.5c, 6.SP.5d**]

Directions: Read and answer each question.

Statistical Questions

1 Which is a statistical question?

Ⓐ How tall am I?

Ⓑ How tall are you?

Ⓒ How many people in this school are over 8 feet tall?

Ⓓ How much did the principal's height increase over the last year?

Think It Through

A statistical question is one for which there are a variety of different correct answers rather than one single answer. For **example 1**, suppose Owen asked each of the questions to 30 people in his school. For which question would there be a variety of different answers?

Measures of Center

2 Jeremy plotted the lengths of 12 adult western coral snakes on this line plot.

```
                X   X
    X           X   X   X
    X   X       X   X   X       X
    13  14  15  16  17  18  19  20  21
```

Length in Inches

Find the mean of the snake lengths.

Ⓐ 17 in.

Ⓑ 17.25 in.

Ⓒ 17.5 in.

Ⓓ 18 in.

Step-By-Step

To find the mean in **example 2**, first add all the lengths. Then, divide by the number of snakes.

1 Add the snake lengths.

14 + 14 + 15 + 17 + 17 + 17 + 18

+ 18 + 18 + 19 + 19 + 21 = ⬜

2 Count the X's to find the number of snakes.

There are ⬜ snakes.

3 Divide the sum by the number of snakes.

⬜ ÷ ⬜ = ⬜

GO ON

Measures of Center

3 Eight students kept track of the number of minutes they spent on a homework assignment.

46	82	42	83	44	83	43	85

What is the median number of minutes spent on the assignment?

Answer: _____

Mean, Median, and Mode

Mean, median, and **mode** describe the center of a set of data that is collected to answer a statistical question.

The **mean**, or average, is the sum of a group of numbers divided by the number in the group.

The **median** is the middle number when the numbers are arranged in order. If there are two middle numbers, then find their mean.

The **mode** is the most frequently occurring number or numbers. There can be no mode, one mode, or more than one mode.

4 Tony's test scores on 8 tests are listed below.

70, 85, 90, 85, 90, 95, 70, 85

What is the mode of the test scores?

- Ⓐ 70
- Ⓑ 85
- Ⓒ 90
- Ⓓ 95

Step-By-Step

There are eight numbers in the data for **example 3**. To find the median, find the mean of the two middle numbers.

1 Put the numbers in order from least to greatest. Circle the two middle numbers.

42, 43, 44, 46, 82, 83, 83, 85

2 Add the two middle numbers and divide the sum by 2. This is the median.

$46 + 82 =$ ▢

▢ $\div 2 =$ ▢

Think It Through

The **mode** is the number that occurs the most in a data set. You need to determine the mode in **example 4**.

Make a tally chart of the numbers.

70	/ /
85	
90	
95	

The mode is ▢.

Measures of Variation

5 The number of minutes that Carrie watched television each day last week is shown below.

90, 150, 120, 180, 60, 240, 90

What is the range of the number of minutes?

Answer: _____

6 The number of birds at Mario's feeder at 10:00 a.m. for the last 5 days is:

13, 17, 8, 12, 20

What is the mean absolute deviation for the data?

Answer: _____

Remember . . .

Range and mean absolute deviation are two measures of variation. They measure how spread out a set of data is.

Range is the difference between the least number and the greatest number in a data set. The greater the range, the more spread out the data is.

Mean absolute deviation is the average amount data points are from the mean. The smaller the number, the more consistent the data is.

Step-By-Step

In **example 5**, you need to determine the **range** of a data set. The range is the difference between the greatest and the least numbers in a data set.

1 Identify the greatest and least numbers.

Greatest: ☐

Least: ☐

2 Subtract.

☐ − ☐ = ☐ minutes

Step-By-Step

For **example 6**, you need to find the average amount each count is from the mean.

1 Find the mean.

$$13 + 17 + 8 + 12 + 20 = \boxed{}$$

$$\boxed{} \div 5 = \boxed{}$$

2 Subtract the mean from each number, then find the absolute value of the difference.

$13 - 14 = -1$	$\lvert-1\rvert = \boxed{}$
$17 - 14 = 3$	$\lvert3\rvert = \boxed{}$
$8 - 14 = -6$	$\lvert-6\rvert = \boxed{}$
$12 - 14 = -2$	$\lvert-2\rvert = \boxed{}$
$20 - 14 = 6$	$\lvert6\rvert = \boxed{}$

3 Find the mean of the absolute values. It tells you the average amount each count deviates from the mean.

$$1 + 3 + 6 + 2 + 6 = \boxed{}$$

$$18 \div 5 = \boxed{}$$

GO ON

Below are the ages of the people who work at a pizza restaurant. Use the set of ages for questions 1–5.

Venucci's Pizza Parlor				
Ages of Employees				
18	23	31	34	17
21	20	23	27	35

1 The sum of the ages of the employees is 249. How can you use this sum to find the mean age?

Ⓐ Divide 249 by 5.

Ⓑ Divide 249 by 10.

Ⓒ Subtract 17 from 35.

Ⓓ Find the middle age when the ages are put in order from least to greatest.

2 What is the range of the ages?

Answer: _____

3 What is the mode?

Answer: _____

4 What is the median?

Answer: _____

5 If the company hires another person, does the median age change?

Ⓐ Yes.

Ⓑ No.

Ⓒ It depends on the number of people who work for the company.

Ⓓ It depends on the age of the person who is hired.

Sari's school cleaned up the city parks. Use the data on the graph for questions 6–8.

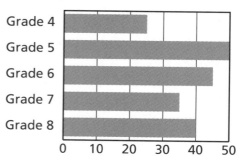

Bags of Trash Collected

6 How many modes does this data set have?

Ⓐ none   Ⓒ 2

Ⓑ 1   Ⓓ 5

7 Find the mean (average) number of bags collected.

Answer: _____

8 The third grade collected 30 bags of trash. If you add this information to the graph, how does the median number of bags change?

Ⓐ It increases.

Ⓑ It decreases.

Ⓒ It doubles.

Ⓓ It stays the same.

Try It *continued*

Below are the test scores of some students on a history test. Use the set of scores for questions 9–12.

History Test Scores
65 70 75 70 80
80 95 60 70 65

9 What is the mean score?

Answer: _____

10 How many students have scores that are above average? (Use the mean.)

Ⓐ 3   Ⓒ 5
Ⓑ 4   Ⓓ 6

11 What is the median score?

Ⓐ 67.5   Ⓒ 72.5
Ⓑ 70   Ⓓ 75

12 What is the mode?

Answer: _____

GO ON

Displaying and Summarizing Data

7 Nigel recorded the number of math problems he did for homework each day for 2 weeks. His results are shown below.

27	36	25	31	34
47	27	25	29	35

Draw a box-and-whisker plot to show the data.

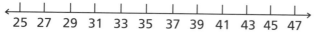

What is the interquartile range for this set of data?

Answer: _____

Box Plots

Box plots separate a data set into quarters. The box encloses the two middle quarters.

Interquartile Range

The interquartile range tells the range of the middle half of a set of data. It is the difference between the upper and lower quartiles.

Upper Quartile – Lower Quartile = Interquartile Range

Step-By-Step

1 To answer **example 7**, order the data from least to greatest.

25, 25, 27, 27, 29, 31, 34, 35, 36, 47

2 Identify the lower and upper extremes—the least and greatest values.

Lower extreme: ☐

Upper extreme: ☐

3 Find the median. This set of data has an even number of values, so find the average of the middle two numbers.

25, 25, 27, 27, **29**, **31**, 34, 35, 36, 47

Median: ☐

4 Find the lower quartile—the median of the lower half of the data.

25, 25, **27**, 27, 29

5 Find the upper quartile—the median of the upper half of the data.

31, 34, **35**, 36, 47

6 On the number line, put a dot above the lower and upper extremes. Draw vertical lines above the median, the lower quartile, and the upper quartile.

7 Complete the plot as shown below.

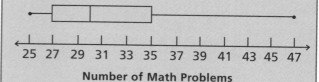

Number of Math Problems

8 Subtract the lower quartile from the upper quartile to find the interquartile range.

35 − 27 = ☐

Displaying and Summarizing Data

8 The histogram below shows the frequency of scores on a math test.

Scores on Math Test

How many test scores are recorded on the graph in all?

Ⓐ 5

Ⓑ 18

Ⓒ 29

Ⓓ 100

Remember . . .

A **histogram** is a frequency graph.

Each bar in a histogram shows a range of data.

Drawing a Histogram

Divide one scale into equal ranges that include all of the data.

Mark the other scale to show frequency.

Count the number of data that fit into each range.

Draw a bar showing the frequency for each range.

Label both scales and title the histogram.

GO ON

9 These are the shoe sizes for each member of the baseball team.

11, 9, 10, 10, 12, 11, 10, 15,

12, 12, 9, 11, 9, 10, 12, 11

Which distribution shape BEST describes this data?

Ⓐ Skewed

Ⓑ Uniform with an outlier

Ⓒ Normal with an outlier

Ⓓ Multiple Peaks

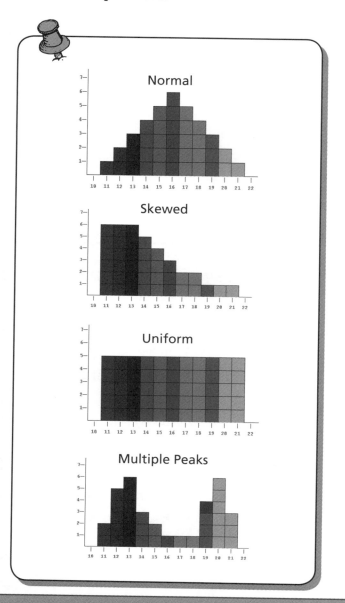

Step-By-Step

To see the shape of the data in **example 9**, display it in a dot plot.

1 Identify the smallest and largest shoe sizes.

Smallest size: ☐

Largest size: ☐

2 Draw a horizontal line and number it to include all of the sizes. Place a mark above the shoe size for each player.

```
        O     O     O
  O     O     O     O
  O     O     O     O
  O     O     O     O                O
  9    10    11    12   13   14   15
```

3 The data shows about the same number of each size shoe except for one size 15 shoe. A number that is much greater or smaller than the rest of the data is called an **outlier**. Look at the distribution shapes in the box to the left. Select the answer that best describes the distribution of the data.

Below are the mean temperatures for a 7-day period. Use the temperatures for questions 13–16.

Mean Temperatures						
Sun	**Mon**	**Tues**	**Wed**	**Thurs**	**Fri**	**Sat**
55°	48°	23°	55°	52°	49°	55°

13 Put the temperatures in order from least to greatest.

Answer: _____

14 Which temperature in the chart is an outlier?

Answer: _____

15 Which of these does NOT change if the outlier is eliminated?

  Ⓐ mean
  Ⓑ median
  Ⓒ mode
  Ⓓ They all change.

16 Which of these changes the most if the outlier is eliminated?

  Ⓐ mean
  Ⓑ median
  Ⓒ mode
  Ⓓ None of them change.

This line plot shows the ages of children attending a day care center. Use the line plot for questions 17–19.

Dandy Day Care Center Ages of Children

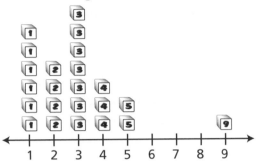

17 Which age is the outlier?

Answer: _____

18 What happens to the mean if the outlier is eliminated?

  Ⓐ It increases.
  Ⓑ It decreases.
  Ⓒ It stays the same.
  Ⓓ It depends on the number of children included on the line plot.

19 What happens to the median if the outlier is eliminated?

Answer: _____

GO ON

20 Over the last five years, the people in the computer club numbered 16, 21, 93, 18, and 15. Which better represents the data, the median or the mean?

Answer: _____

21 For which set of heights are the mean, median, and mode the same? All heights are in inches.

Ⓐ 68, 68, 68, 68, 68, 68, 68

Ⓑ 60, 61, 62, 63, 64, 65, 66

Ⓒ 60, 65, 65, 65, 65, 65, 68

Ⓓ 60, 60, 60, 65, 68, 68, 68

22 Thirty students were asked how many books they read last month.

Books Read Last Month
0 0 1 1 1 2 2 2 2 2 3 3 3 3 3
3 3 3 3 3 3 3 3 3 4 4 4 5 5 12

Choose the BEST description of this data.

Ⓐ No one student read a lot more books than anyone else.

Ⓑ The students read about 3 books each.

Ⓒ Everyone read fewer than 12 books.

Ⓓ The students read 1 or more books each.

23 Ramon's math scores for the first semester are shown below. Draw a box-and-whisker plot to show the data.

82   98   76   86   85

74   56   100   98   97

Interquartile range: _____

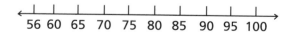

56 60 65 70 75 80 85 90 95 100

Open-Ended Practice

Some tests include open-ended questions in which you must show your work and write an explanation of the steps you took. There is often more than one answer or more than one way to find a solution to these problems.

Displaying and Summarizing Data

10 Victor drew this line plot to show the heights of the players on his favorite football team.

Ravens Football Team

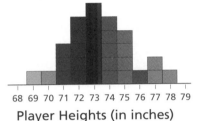

68 69 70 71 72 73 74 75 76 77 78 79
Player Heights (in inches)

Describe what the graph shows and summarize the data.

Explanation: _____

_____

_____

_____

_____

_____

_____

_____

Step-By-Step

To describe the data shown in the line plot for **example 10**, first look at the title and the units of measure used. Identify the number of players. Then summarize the data by looking at its shape and telling about the center and variation of the data.

My Plan: *First I will name the topic of the graph, the units used, and the number of data. Then I will find the shape, range, median, mode, and mean to summarize the data.*

1 Describe the data.

The line plot shows the heights of ☐ football players.

The heights are measured in ☐ .

2 Summarize the data.

The heights are about normally distributed with most players between

71 and ☐ inches tall.

The shortest player is ☐ inches.

The tallest player is ☐ inches.

The range of the heights is 78 − 69 = ☐ inches.

The median height is ☐ inches.

The mean height is 2,128 ÷ 29 = ☐ inches.

The mode is ☐ inches.

Explanation: *The line plot label told me that the heights of the football players were measured in inches. I counted squares to find that 29 players were measured. Next, I observed that the data forms a normal distribution shape. Then I subtracted the least height from the greatest height to find that the range is 9 inches. Since there are 29 players, the median height is the 15th number, 73. The most common height is 73 inches, so that is the mode. I added the heights of each player and divided by the number of players to find that the mean height is about 73.4 inches.*

Unit 7 Application

11 Rashad is analyzing the circumferences of trees that have survived a recent forest fire. The following are the circumferences in inches of the 12 trees he measured: 26, 34, 28, 20, 63, 42, 28, 65, 66, 87, 18, 51.

When he submits his report he needs to provide the mean, median, mode, range, and any outliers. Then he needs to create a box-and-whisker plot to show the trends of the tree sizes graphically. Help Rashad by finding each of the items he is looking for and then completing the box-and-whisker plot.

Step 1

18, _____ , 26, _____ , _____ ,

34, _____ , 51, 63, 65, _____ , _____

Step 2

_____ + _____ + _____ + _____ + _____ + _____ + _____

_____ + _____ + _____ + _____ + _____ = _____

_____ ÷ 12 = _____.

The mean is _____ inches.

Step 3

$$\underset{\substack{\text{middle} \\ \text{number}}}{\underline{\hspace{1.5cm}}} + \underset{\substack{\text{middle} \\ \text{number}}}{\underline{\hspace{1.5cm}}} = \underset{\text{total}}{\underline{\hspace{1.5cm}}} ÷ 2 = \underset{\substack{\text{average of} \\ \text{two middle} \\ \text{numbers}}}{\underline{\hspace{1.5cm}}}$$

Step 4

Only one number occurs twice, and that is _____.

So _____ inches is the mode.

Step-By-Step

1 In order to find each of the items required and complete the box-and-whisker plot, I will want to begin by putting the numbers in order from least to greatest.

2 First, I will find the mean. I do this by adding all of the numbers and dividing by the sample size.

3 I will find the median next. I have an even number of trees in my sample, so I will take the middle two numbers from Step 1.

Now, I need to find the average of the middle two numbers.

4 Now I'll find the mode.

Unit 7 Application *continued*

Step 5

_____ − _____ = _____ .
highest   lowest   range
number   number

The range of the numbers is _____ inches.

Step 6

_____ appears to be an outlier, because it is so much larger than the rest.

Step 7

We draw the line from smallest circumference to the largest circumference, excluding the outlier. We add a dot above the outlier.

We mark the median.

We use the median of the first half of the data and mark the lower quartile. We use the median of the second half of the data to mark the upper quartile.

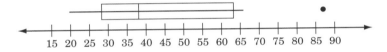

Step-By-Step

5 For the range I take the highest number and subtract the lowest number.

6 Last of all I will look for any outliers.

7 Now I will complete our box-and-whisker plot.

Now Robbie can submit his findings on the trees that survived the forest fire.

24 Harry has taken measurements of eight of his classmates' feet. The following are the measurements in inches of 8 of his classmates: 13, 12, 8, 9, 8, 7, 14, 9. Find the mean, median, mode, range, and any outliers. Then graph using a histogram or box-and-whisker plot.

Mean: _____

Median: _____

Mode: _____

Range: _____

Outliers: _____

25 Eliza is doing a survey of the number of televisions in 7 of her classmates' homes. The homes she surveyed had the following number of TVs: 3, 1, 3, 2, 0, 8, 2. Find the mean, median, mode, range, and any outliers. Then graph using a histogram or box-and-whisker plot.

Mean: _____

Median: _____

Mode: _____

Range: _____

Outliers: _____

26 Bridget is gathering information on high scores in a recent bowling match with her 5 friends. Their scores were: 165, 200, 215, 285, 170. Find the mean, median, mode, range, and any outliers. Then graph using a box-and-whisker plot.

Mean: _____

Median: _____

Mode: _____

Range: _____

Outliers: _____

Go for it!

Test Practice 7: Statistics

Estimated time: 30 minutes

Directions: Read and answer each question.

Use the table to answer questions 1–3.

Day	Cones Sold
Sunday	59
Monday	52
Tuesday	37
Wednesday	37
Thursday	37
Friday	70
Saturday	92

1 What is the mode of the number of cones sold?

Ⓐ 33
Ⓑ 37
Ⓒ 52
Ⓓ 55

2 What is the median number of cones sold?

Answer: _____

3 What is the range of the number of cones sold?

Ⓐ 33
Ⓑ 37
Ⓒ 52
Ⓓ 55

Use this graph for questions 4 and 5.

4 Which best describes the distribution of the data?

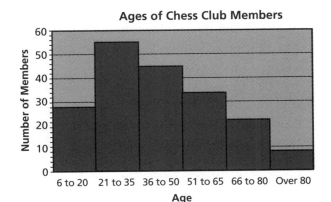

Ages of Chess Club Members

Ⓐ Skewed
Ⓑ Multiple Peaks
Ⓒ Uniform
Ⓓ Normal

5 Write the statistical question Shontelle asked to gather the data shown.

Answer: _____

6 Which does NOT describe the center of a set of data?

Ⓐ mean
Ⓑ mode
Ⓒ range
Ⓓ median

GO ON ➡

Dora's bowling scores this week were: 152, 170, 161.
Use the scores to answer questions 7 and 8.

7 What was Dora's mean score?

Answer: _____

8 What is the mean absolute deviation for the scores?

Answer: _____

The box-and-whisker plot shows the number of baskets Carl made during each game last season. Use it to answer questions 9 and 10.

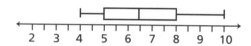

9 What is the range of the number of baskets Carl made?

Answer: _____

10 What is the interquartile range?

Answer: _____

Use the two line plots below for question 11.

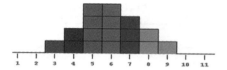

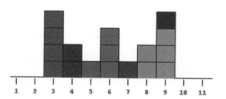

11 Which statement is NOT true?

 Ⓐ Both data sets have the same median.

 Ⓑ Both data sets have the same range.

 Ⓒ Both data sets have the same mean.

 Ⓓ Both data sets have the same mode.

12 Mandy scored 88, 94, 82, and 89 on her math tests. What is the lowest score she can earn on her next math test to have a mean of 90 or more?

Answer: _____

13 This box plot shows the finish times for the first 100 runners in a marathon.

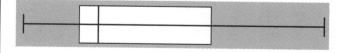

In which quarter of the data are the times closest together?

 Ⓐ First quarter

 Ⓑ Second quarter

 Ⓒ Third quarter

 Ⓓ Fourth quarter

14 Five buckets each had different amounts of water in them. Elka poured all of the water together. She divided the water equally among the 5 buckets. Which term describes the amount of water in each bucket?

Ⓐ mean

Ⓑ range

Ⓒ outlier

Ⓓ mean absolute deviation

15 The table shows the mean and the mean absolute deviation for the weights of 4 groups of 12 pumpkins each.

Group	Mean	Mean Absolute Deviation
A	16	5
B	22	8
C	12	2
D	17	6

For which group of pumpkins are the weights of all of the pumpkins in the group closest to the mean?

Ⓐ A

Ⓑ B

Ⓒ C

Ⓓ D

16 Marcie asked 20 members of an orchestra how old they were when they first played with an orchestra.

Age of debut with an orchestra:

9, 11, 6, 9, 12, 17, 12, 11, 13, 15, 11,

18, 11, 11, 14, 12, 15, 14, 8, 11

Draw a box plot to show the data.

Complete this list of measures for the data:

Lower extreme: _____

Upper extreme: _____

Median: _____

Lower quartile: _____

Upper quartile: _____

Range: _____

Interquartile range: _____

Number Correct/Total = _____ /16

Mastery Test

Estimated time: 60 minutes

Directions: Read and answer each question.

1 There were 80 tickets sold for the class play. Of these, 24 were adults and the rest were children. Write the ratio of adults to children in simplest form.

Ⓐ $\frac{3}{7}$
Ⓑ $\frac{7}{3}$
Ⓒ $\frac{3}{10}$
Ⓓ $\frac{7}{10}$

2 Tomas made 10 birdhouses in $2\frac{1}{2}$ hours. At what unit rate did he make birdhouses?

Answer: _____ per hour

3 Together Reggie and Beverly picked 72 flowers. Reggie picked 5 flowers for every 3 flowers Beverly picked. How many flowers did Beverly pick? Show your work below.

Answer: _____

4 Malory rode her bicycle 54 miles in 4.5 hours. At that rate, how far can she ride in 6 hours?

Answer: _____

5 Thirty-six out of the 60 trees Nick planted were pine trees. What percent of the trees were pine trees?

Answer: _____

6 The table shows the ratio of minutes to pages printed for a copy machine.

Minutes	Copies Made
5	75
10	150
15	
20	300

What number is missing in the table?

Answer: _____

7 Chloe got a 10% raise. She now earns $22 an hour. How much did she earn per hour before the raise?

Answer: _____

8 A bicycle regularly priced at $396 is on sale for 25% off. What is the sale price?

Answer: _____

9 Which measure is equal to 350 meters?

Ⓐ 0.035 km
Ⓑ 0.35 km
Ⓒ 35 km
Ⓓ 3,500 km

10 This diagram shows how many pieces of copper wire $\frac{1}{8}$ yard long can be cut from a roll of wire that is $\frac{3}{4}$ yard.

$\frac{1}{4}$	$\frac{1}{4}$	$\frac{1}{4}$	$\frac{1}{4}$

$\frac{1}{8}$	$\frac{1}{8}$	$\frac{1}{8}$	$\frac{1}{8}$	$\frac{1}{8}$	$\frac{1}{8}$	$\frac{1}{8}$	$\frac{1}{8}$

Which division equation represents this diagram?

Ⓐ $\frac{3}{4} \div \frac{1}{8} = 6$

Ⓑ $\frac{1}{8} \div \frac{3}{4} = 6$

Ⓒ $\frac{3}{4} \div \frac{1}{8} = \frac{6}{8}$

Ⓓ $\frac{1}{8} \div 6 = \frac{3}{4}$

11 How many $\frac{1}{4}$-pound servings of potatoes can be made from $\frac{7}{8}$ pounds of potatoes?

Answer: _____

12 A box of 945 pencils is divided equally into 35 smaller boxes. How many pencils are in each smaller box? Show your work below.

Ⓐ 25   Ⓒ 207

Ⓑ 27   Ⓓ 910

13 Nathan bought a loaf of bread for $2.79 and some bananas for $1.70. How much change did he get back from $5?

Answer: _____

14 Maureen used 0.9 meters of fabric to make a pillow. How many more pillows of this size can Maureen make with 12.75 meters of additional fabric?

Ⓐ 1.4   Ⓒ 14

Ⓑ 1.5   Ⓓ 15

15 What is the greatest common factor (GCF) of 32 and 17?

Ⓐ 1   Ⓒ 28

Ⓑ 17   Ⓓ 544

16 What is the least common multiple (LCM) of 12 and 9?

Answer: _____

17 Use the distributive property to write 35 + 15 as a sum with no common factors.

Answer: _____

18 Leo returned a part that cost $16.43 to the hardware store. The store credited his charge account. Write the number to show the credit.

Answer: _____

19 Use this number line. What is the opposite of −5 ?

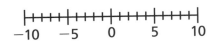

Answer: _____

GO ON

20 In which quadrant is point $(5, -4)$ located?

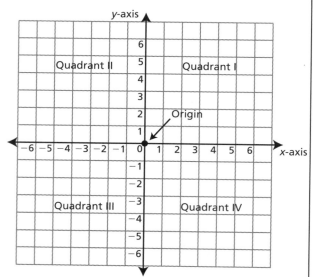

Answer: _____

21 What are the coordinates of the reflection of $(3, -5)$ over the x-axis?

Ⓐ $(3, -5)$

Ⓑ $(-3, 5)$

Ⓒ $(-3, -5)$

Ⓓ $(3, 5)$

22 Which inequality is shown by the points on this number line?

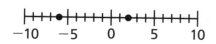

Ⓐ $2 > -6$　　Ⓒ $-2 < -6$

Ⓑ $-6 > 2$　　Ⓓ $2 < 6$

23 Which temperature is greater than $-8°$ Fahrenheit?

Ⓐ $-32°$　　Ⓒ $-1°$

Ⓑ $-9°$　　Ⓓ $-19°$

24 What is $|-3|$?

Answer: _____

25 Use this grid to show the locations of the museums in Springfield.

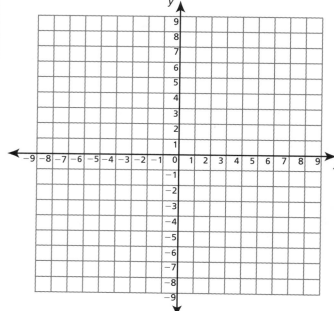

Railroad Museum $(-5, 6)$
Art Museum $(7, 6)$
Natural History Museum $(7, -4)$
Space Museum $(-7, -6)$

Each side of a square shows 1 mile.

A How far is it from the Railroad Museum to the Art Museum?

Answer: _____

B How far is it from the Art Museum to the Natural History Museum?

Answer: _____

26 Which expression equals 6^5?

Ⓐ 5×6

Ⓑ $5 \times 6 \times 5 \times 6 \times 5 \times 6$

Ⓒ $6 \times 6 \times 6 \times 6 \times 6$

Ⓓ $5 \times 5 \times 5 \times 5 \times 5 \times 5$

27 Which expression represents 14 less than three times a number n?

Ⓐ $14 - 3n$　　　Ⓒ $3(14 - n)$

Ⓑ $3n - 14$　　　Ⓓ $3(n - 14)$

28 What is the coefficient of y in the expression $12 + 3y - 2x$?

Answer: _____

29 The formula for the area of a triangle is $A = \frac{1}{2}bh$. Use the formula to find the area of a triangle with a base (b) of 14 centimeters and a height (h) of 20 centimeters.

Ⓐ 17 cm^2　　　Ⓒ 280 cm^2

Ⓑ 140 cm^2　　　Ⓓ 560 cm^2

30 If $x = 5$ and $y = 9$, what is the value of $(x + 5) \times (20 - y)$?

Ⓐ 96　　　Ⓒ 121

Ⓑ 110　　　Ⓓ 210

31 Simplify this expression.

$$18 + 3 \times 16 \div 2^3 - 5$$

Answer: _____

32 Which expression is equivalent to $36x + 60y$?

Ⓐ $12(3x + 5y)$　　　Ⓒ $6(9x + 10y)$

Ⓑ $12(3y + 5x)$　　　Ⓓ $6(6x + 12y)$

33 Simplify this expression.

$$3y + 2y + 7 + y$$

Ⓐ $6y + 7$　　　Ⓒ $4y^2 + 2y + 7$

Ⓑ $12y^2$　　　Ⓓ $3y + 2y + 7$

34 Which value of x makes the inequality $x \le -3$ true?

Ⓐ -5　　　Ⓒ 2

Ⓑ -2　　　Ⓓ 5

35 How can you solve the equation $y - 12 = 15$?

Ⓐ Add 15 to both sides.

Ⓑ Subtract 15 from both sides.

Ⓒ Add 12 to both sides.

Ⓓ Subtract 12 from both sides.

36 Steven bought 3 mirrors. He paid a total of $264. Which equation can be used to find the amount he paid for each mirror?

Ⓐ $3 \times m = \$264$

Ⓑ $\$264 \times m = 3$

Ⓒ $3 \div m = \$264$

Ⓓ $\$264 = m + 3$

37 Solve for p.

$$18 \times p = 108$$

Ⓐ $p = 1,944$　　　Ⓒ $p = 6$

Ⓑ $p = 11$　　　Ⓓ $p = 4$

38 The greatest number of passengers a bus can carry is 54. Write an inequality to show the number of passengers, p.

Answer: _____

39 Which number line shows the solution for the inequality $n < 1$?

Ⓐ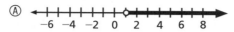

Ⓑ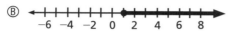

Ⓒ

Ⓓ

40 Find the area of this polygon and explain how you do it.

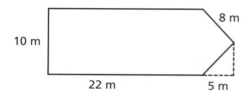

Answer: _____

Explanation: _____

_____

_____

_____

41 Sam is building a table. The figure shows the dimensions of the top of the table. What is the area of the tabletop?

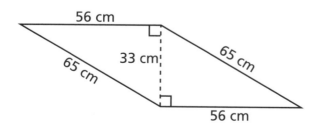

Ⓐ 924 cm²

Ⓑ 1,848 cm²

Ⓒ 2,145 cm²

Ⓓ 3,640 cm²

42 Esmile started a savings account with $50. He recorded the amount in his savings account each month.

Savings

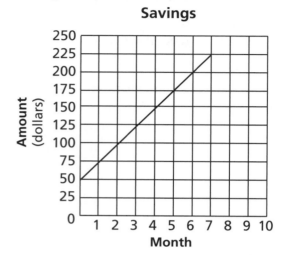

Complete the table to show the relationship between the number of months (m) and the amount of savings (a). Then write an equation. Explain your answer.

Month (*m*)	Amount (*a*)

Answer: _____

Explanation: _____

_____

_____

_____

43 A box of matches is $\frac{1}{2}$ inch tall, $2\frac{1}{4}$ inches long, and $1\frac{1}{2}$ inches wide. What is the volume of the box?

Answer: _____

44 Plot the points $(-5, 2)$, $(4, 2)$, $(4, -5)$, and $(-5, -5)$ on this coordinate grid. Connect the points in order.

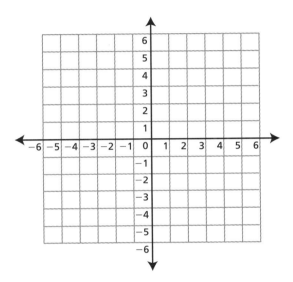

What is the perimeter of the quadrilateral?

Answer: _____

45 Celeste asked the members of her soccer team these questions. Which is a statistical question?

   Ⓐ What size are your soccer shoes?
   Ⓑ What is the date of our next soccer game?
   Ⓒ How many games have we won so far this year?
   Ⓓ What is the most points we have scored in one game this season?

46 Roger made this box in the shape of a triangular prism.

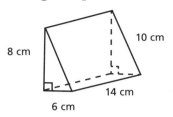

Draw a net of the box. Then find its surface area. Show your work.

Answer: _____

47 Maya recorded these daily high temperatures in degrees Fahrenheit for 10 days.

| 46 | 31 | 33 | 42 | 25 |
| 29 | 37 | 44 | 45 | 36 |

What is the median temperature?

   Ⓐ 25°F   Ⓒ 37°F
   Ⓑ 36.5°F   Ⓓ 46°F

Andy recorded the time it took him to walk to school each day last week. Use his data to answer questions 48–50.

> **Minutes to Walk to School**
>
> 26   24   20   25   25

48 What is the range of the times?

- Ⓐ 26 minutes
- Ⓑ 20 minutes
- Ⓒ 6 minutes
- Ⓓ 5 minutes

49 What is the mean of the times?

- Ⓐ 23 minutes
- Ⓑ 24 minutes
- Ⓒ 25 minutes
- Ⓓ 26 minutes

50 What is the mean absolute deviation for the times?

- Ⓐ 6 minutes
- Ⓑ 5 minutes
- Ⓒ 1.6 minutes
- Ⓓ 0.6 minutes

51 Which describes the spread of a set of data?

- Ⓐ mean
- Ⓑ mode
- Ⓒ range
- Ⓓ median

52 The median price of a house in Brookdale is $243,000. What does the median price tell you about the prices of homes in Brookdale?

- Ⓐ The home prices in Brookdale vary by $243,000.
- Ⓑ The middle price of the homes in Brookdale is $243,000.
- Ⓒ The most frequent price for a home in Brookdale is $243,000.
- Ⓓ The difference between the highest and lowest prices is $243,000.

53 For which box plot are the values for the upper quartile of the data closest together?

The histogram shows the ages of members of a model airplane club. Use the histogram for questions 54 and 55.

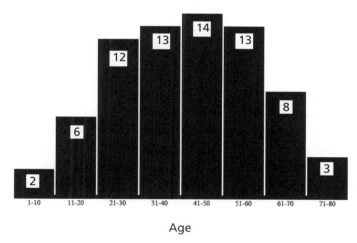

Ages of Model Airplane Club Members

54 How many members does the model airplane club have?

Answer: _____

55 Which describes the shape of the data?

    Ⓐ normal   Ⓒ skewed right with an outlier

    Ⓑ uniform   Ⓓ skewed left with an outlier

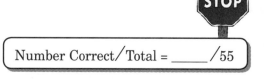

Number Correct/Total = _____/55

Keeping Score

	Points Earned / Total Points	Percent Score
Tryout Test	/55	%
Test Practice 1 Ratios and Proportional Relationships	/22	%
Test Practice 2 Operations	/20	%
Test Practice 3 Number Concepts	/24	%
Test Practice 4 Expressions	/20	%
Test Practice 5 Equations and Inequalities	/20	%
Test Practice 6 Measurement and Geometry	/16	%
Test Practice 7 Statistics	/16	%
Mastery Test	/55	%

1. Fill in the number of points you earned in the Points Earned box.

2. Use the Finding Percent chart on page 135 to figure out your Percent Score. Then fill in the % box.

3. Compare your Percent Scores for the Tryout Test and the Mastery Test. See how much you've learned!

Finding Percent

Many tests give your score in both number of points earned and in percentages. This handy chart will tell you your percent score.

1. Find the band with the same number of points that are on your test.
2. Follow along the top row of the band to the number of points you earned. Your percent score is right below it.

‑ ‑ ‑ Number of Points on Test

16

1	2	3	4	5	6	7	8	9	10	11	12	13	14	15	16
6%	13%	19%	25%	31%	38%	44%	50%	56%	63%	69%	75%	81%	88%	94%	100%

20

1	2	3	4	5	6	7	8	9	10	11	12	13	14	15	16
5%	10%	15%	20%	25%	30%	35%	40%	45%	50%	55%	60%	65%	70%	75%	80%

17	18	19	20
85%	90%	95%	100%

22

1	2	3	4	5	6	7	8	9	10	11	12	13	14	15	16	17	18	19	20	21	22
5%	9%	14%	18%	23%	27%	32%	36%	41%	45%	50%	55%	60%	64%	68%	73%	77%	82%	86%	91%	95%	100%

24

1	2	3	4	5	6	7	8	9	10	11	12	13	14	15	16
4%	8%	13%	17%	21%	25%	29%	33%	38%	42%	46%	50%	54%	58%	63%	67%

17	18	19	20	21	22	23	24
71%	75%	79%	83%	88%	92%	96%	100%

55

1	2	3	4	5	6	7	8	9	10	11	12	13	14	15	16	17	18
2%	4%	5%	7%	9%	11%	13%	15%	16%	18%	20%	22%	24%	25%	27%	29%	31%	33%

19	20	21	22	23	24	25	26	27	28	29	30	31	32	33	34	35	36
35%	36%	38%	40%	42%	44%	45%	47%	49%	51%	53%	55%	56%	58%	60%	62%	64%	65%

37	38	39	40	41	42	43	44	45	46	47	48	49	50	51	52	53	54	55
67%	69%	71%	73%	75%	76%	78%	80%	82%	84%	85%	87%	89%	91%	93%	95%	96%	98%	100%